PICK OF The Oldie

OLDIE PUBLICATIONS

'I'm an MP. What's in it for me?'

Published by Oldie Publications Ltd
65 Newman Street, London W1T 3EG
www.theoldie.co.uk

Copyright © 2013 Oldie Publications Ltd

ISBN: 978-1-901170-20-7

A catalogue record for this book is available from the British Library

Printed and bound in the UK by Butler Tanner & Dennis Ltd

Acknowledgements
The Oldie would like to thank all the writers, illustrators
and cartoonists whose work is reproduced in these pages

Designed by Joe Buckley and John Bowling

PICK OF The Oldie

FROM THE LAST 21 YEARS

EDITED BY SONALI CHAPMAN

CONTENTS

My life with GARBO

A flight of fancy by American novelist **PATRICIA HIGHSMITH**

Illustration by JIMMY THOMSON

I hasten to say that I never met Greta Garbo. But I came close to it several times in New York in the late 1940s and early 1950s, when I had a flat at First Avenue and 56th Street, in a building on the north-west corner, to be exact. Greta Garbo lived 'somewhere' in the East 50s, and three or four times a year I would glimpse her, striding along in dark clothes usually, head bent under a broad-brimmed hat that was usually black. Of course, I stopped and stared, if she was across the street or avenue, or even on the same pavement. Staring could not have bothered her, because she never looked round at anybody. Always she was in flat shoes, and usually a loose coat with collar

turned up, as if to conceal more of her face than the hat did. Sometimes she carried a small sack, as if she had bought a sweater or a book, but not groceries. I never attempted to follow her, never saw her with anyone.

There was a time when I nearly met her in the sense of bumping into her. This was at the south-east corner of Fifth Avenue and 57th Street, which had a sharp and windowless angle, because of a big office building there, so that anyone coming round it at normal speed and encountering someone coming from the opposite direction would collide with that person, and this I nearly did one windy afternoon, jumping back just in time. It was Greta Garbo, all in black, with

the famous hat on, too. How thrilled I was – though I hadn't touched her, or exchanged a glance, much less a smile. I remember turning and watching her clump off purposefully downtown on Fifth Avenue.

'Do you know I almost bumped into *Greta Garbo* this afternoon?' I remember telling someone that evening, smiling proudly.

'Did you? How? *Where?*... What was she wearing?... How tall is she?'

'A little taller than me.'

'Did her feet look so big?'

'Not for her height. I came within inches –! Sort of embarrassing,' I went on, pleased as Punch.

How easy it would have been to embroider, to say that we had a collision, that Greta Garbo rubbed her nose, laughed quickly, and said with a heavy Swedish accent, 'Ooo-ooh, my fault! Sor-ry!'

'Oh, no, *my* fault,' I would have insisted politely, and then we would have gone on our ways. This conversation would have been like a biblical episode in which a recently deceased person is wished to reappear, and so he or she does, and maybe even says a few words. The narrator knows he is stretching things, but after a few recountings comes to believe it absolutely himself.

However, there was no doubt that Garbo did exist in what I called my neighbourhood. I saw her also – but rarely of course – when I drifted along Third Avenue and gazed into the cluttered windows of antique shops. One could buy a charming egg-cup from England or France, for instance, for a dollar. For twenty dollars I acquired a Victorian stereopticon plus at least two hundred marvellous old photographs from the 1880s to about 1910 to go with it. If I saw Garbo on Third Avenue, I never saw her raptly gazing, as I did, but always hurrying along, looking at the pavement, only her nose visible under her hat, perhaps a hand clasping the coat closer about her rather lanky figure. Still, it was a day when I could say to myself and others, 'Guess what, I saw Greta Garbo today!'

This was of course not the same as living with Garbo, merely to have a dwelling in her neighbourhood, as I had. Now, however, in a different sense (Garbo is dead, after all), I feel that I do live with her, because I have a delicately coloured drawing – water-colour, pen and ink, grey, yellow and sepia wash – from the Greta Garbo Collection, framed and hanging in my bedroom-workroom. This drawing was auctioned by Sotheby's in New York a couple of years ago, bought and sent to me by an acquaintance now living in the United States. He enclosed no comment on the drawing.

It is some nine-and-a-half inches wide and twelve inches high, and shows a gentleman of the Louis XV period with long brown (sepia) wig, dark hat, long beige coat with buttons down the front, cane and slipper (only one is showing) with buckle and heel, about to get into his waiting carriage, the back half of which, with curtained window,

is evidenced in the background. He is bidding adieu to, or being bidden adieu by, a most affectionate-looking figure in black wearing a brimmed black hat, who presses against him and rests a hand delicately upon the gentleman's left forearm. This erect figure in black has blondish straight hair of more than shoulder length, and the question which arises almost instantly on looking at this composition is, is the figure in black a young woman or man? The hand of the young person (younger than the gentleman who has two creases down his cheek, partly caused by his faint smile) looks feminine, but so do the hands of the older gentleman, whose right hand rests upon the head of his cane, and the left just above his left thigh, as if he is in doubt whether to take the hand of the figure in black. They gaze closely at each other, and with knowing smiles.

In the background, greyish rooftops silhouette themselves against the sky, there are two steeples, the higher bearing a cross. Between the carriage and the rooftops, a few trees are indicated in pale wash. The two figures are hidden from any viewer on the church side by the tall body of the carriage. Some words are written in pencil below this composition, on a paper mat on which the drawing itself has been pasted:

> 'and when he went from London,
>   he said he believed
> he should never come to town more.'

The handwriting is quite legible and even simple.

Could Garbo have written those words herself, made them up or copied them from some favourite poem or story? Where did this drawing come from? Shall I make an effort to find out, or live with it as I do now (I've had it about two months), enjoying the wanderings of fancy?

That there is a sexual business between the two figures is in no doubt. The slender figure in black could be twenty or eighteen. The bewigged gentleman, elegantly slim though he is, is certainly forty. The pronouns in the pencilled statement are masculine. The real ambiguity is in the beautiful face of the blond figure, which except for a strong jaw appears female. The interesting question to me is, did Greta Garbo buy or acquire this drawing somehow, because the figure with the longish blond hair looked like herself?

I confess that is what I prefer to believe. The young blond-haired figure in black suggests to me the Garbo I saw so many times in Manhattan. The mouth certainly, close-lipped and slightly smiling, resembles Garbo's. A curve of black trousers suggests a feminine hip, though this could be caused by a tight belt. The height of the two appears the same; the blond-haired figure looms slightly taller, because the older man is about to take a big step (with the aid of a walking stick) to a cement slab of some kind which will put him on a level to enter his carriage.

If one stands back from the drawing, the figure in black dominates the composition. Because of the pavement rise at the knee level of this figure, and the grey-stockinged lower left leg of the older gentleman, the dark trousers are partly obscured at ankle level, suggesting that the younger man has unusually long feet – but only from a distance. This is an intimate picture, however, asking for close examination.

Did a contemporary of Garbo – an artist friend or acquaintance – create this little picture for her as a spoof, a private joke? This is probably exactly what she would have liked and preferred. Something the public would never know about, private laughter, delight, pleasure. A thing of beauty, really, to glance at every day or every other day, as she entered her bedroom, for instance.

Patricia Highsmith

Towards the upper left corner of the drawing, printed by hand, vertically, are the letters INGRE but with no final S, and the N is written backward, in sepia wash against the greyish wash of the sky. The letters are as faint as a watermark. Is the amateur or the art historian to pay attention to INGRE, try to determine provenance? Is it another joke between the artist and Greta Garbo?

And since it was rumoured about Garbo that she preferred women – easy to rumour as she never married – the composition in question could be a double joke. If the figure in black is female, the tableau becomes quite proper. Yet this supposition is made dubious by the pencilled statement below, with its masculine pronouns.

The mind wanders, or mine does, to Garbo films, her often unsmiling and rather cold face lifted like a ship's figurehead in a *Catherine the Great* poster, for instance. Garbo laughs – in *Ninotchka* – and the world heard it! One of the wonders of the twentieth century. *Anna Karenina* demanded passion, duplicity, a burst of bliss, finally tragedy. Garbo made it – herself unique and untouchable somehow, even by the male lovers who embraced her.

I can never forget – and I can hear this too – Garbo's voice saying, 'I vant to be alone' in a deep and earnest tone that meant to any hearer: Garbo speaks the truth. That statement may be the most certain thing anyone will ever be able to say about Garbo. Some of her contemporaries in Sweden may have known her well, fairly well, or only slightly. There was an altercation after her death about who inherited. The newspapers mentioned a nephew who was to have been the main inheritor, and I think he finally was.

One imagines Garbo living in Manhattan, seeing a very small circle of friends. When the telephone rang, it would have been one of this circle. She evidently preferred New York, with the anonymity afforded by its swarming eight million, to the more sparsely populated Sweden and Stockholm. I hope she had Swedish salmon flown in sometimes, pressed between ice slabs with salt and sugar and the herb called *til*, plucked from the highest mountain slopes. One can only imagine her telephone bills. How nice to imagine Garbo laughing – and lifting her lidded eyes to the drawing

I'm describing, gazing at the mysterious androgyne in black with his delicate hand pressing the gentleman's puffed silk sleeve with a light touch that implies the heaviest of passions.

Garbo laughs on the telephone! 'Come for some champagne and a supper tonight. I don't vant to be alone.'

> **Could Garbo have written those words herself, made them up or copied them from a favourite poem?**

Neither do the two in the drawing. And what have they been doing that afternoon, or the preceding night? The sky is rather clear, no indication of dusk. What time is it? Do lovers ever know? There is one thing definite about the words: they are a farewell, and a sad one, only mitigated by the tender smile on the lips of each.

Did Greta Garbo speculate in the same vein about these two?

'This is our last evening – shouldn't we make more of it?'

'Why? – You know I'll remember you forever – all my life – after I die –'

'You make me die a little now.'

'Your carriage – Dismiss that damned coachman!'

'Not so loud.'

No, quieter. Both faces show closed lips.

Did Garbo ever ask a friend – on seeing him or her gazing at the drawing, 'What do you think? Is the figure in black a boy or a gir-rl?'

It is possible that the reply would be, 'A girl – in disguise?'

'This one's called Recession because he never goes away'

This presents a new scenario: the older gentleman (though married) is enamoured of a beautiful young woman in London, whom he has to meet secretly. Perhaps the gentleman has rented an apartment especially for this purpose, and the young woman has to come to the apartment, and departs, in male attire for safety's sake.

Or – the possibilities are many – the gentleman prefers his females in male attire, being in love with his own fantasies too.

Then we have, 'and when he went from London, he said he believed he should never come to town more', a statement made by the gentleman about himself, and the 'should' takes on prudence rather than being merely a subjunctive.

But there remains the height, the strong jaw of the figure in black to argue for its being a male form. Plus the clothing, of course.

Now the picture hangs in a corner of my room, over a low green-painted chest of drawers, and near a bookcase. The young man in black faces inward to the room. Soon I shall hang it in the living-room, where more people will see it. I long to hear the comments, even to remark the silences, the blank glances that have brought nothing to the viewer's brain. Some people are blind to any kind of pictures – not usually my friends, but then all sorts of people come to my house. My friends usually notice everything, and they love to comment.

'Garbo! – How interesting – that she owned it. Looks sort of like Garbo here, don't you think?'

I would like to think that Garbo could hear such remarks from another world, from on high or wherever she is, but since I don't believe in consciousness after death, I cannot indulge in that fantasy. I simply imagine, knowing I'm making it all up, that Garbo, having much liked this drawing, takes an interest now in what people say, and laughs at or troubles to consider an interpretation of 'The Farewell at the Carriage' – my title.

Thank you, Greta Garbo, wherever you are. Thank you for your films, your style, your beauty. Thank you for managing to stay alone, for the most part, not easy for people in your profession. After me, your picture will be passed on into good hands; with my request, keep passing it on into good hands.

Joanna Lumley

picks her top six

1. Elvis Presley
I don't know what pin-up means unless it is Elvis. The absolute rock'n'roll star, the ultimate idol. Also called interviewers 'Sir': the combo of courtesy and cool is a killer.

2. John Betjeman
Some of his poetry seems the best ever written. 'Business Girls' is my fave.

3. Barry Humphries
Sandy, Les and Edna are also my pin-ups – particularly Sandy who has a lot in common with Betjeman.

4. Jean Muir
Everything that can be said about style or taste or fashion, Jean was there first – with effortless ease and matchless superiority.

5. Gioachino Rossini
He wanted to be a cook but his family wouldn't let him. To be a musician of that calibre as your *second* string – cool beyond belief.

6. Dame Freya Stark
If I could travel like that and write like that, I'd die a happy person. Actually I'm happy anyway, but I'd die a more *fabulous* person.

PIN-UPS

TIM ROOKE/REX FEATURES

Left: Joanna Lumley

OFF THE RAILS

A MASTER'S VOICE

HAVE YOU EVER wondered what it's like to hear your name called over BR's public address system? You know the sort of thing. 'Would Mr David Ransom, a passenger from Ipswich, please call at the Station Master's office.' I'm giving away my age by referring to the Station Master's office. The modern exhortation to 'go to the Information Desk' doesn't have quite the same ring to it. You feel you are to be dealt with by a mere clerk, whereas an invitation to the Station Master's office implies that the information to be imparted is of such dire importance that only the Station Master himself – top-hat and all – can deal with it. Nothing less than death or disaster could occasion such an announcement, and to hear one's name wafting about the lofty magnificence of Liverpool Street station is very disconcerting. If for no reason other than that you feel the eyes of everyone there are upon you. It has happened to me twice.

> *I heard above the hiss and clamour of Liverpool Street, 'Will Master David Ransom please go to the Station Master's office'*

The first occasion was many years ago. I was a boarder at a London choir school, and my parents mistook the day I was due back at school. There can be few greater pleasures for a nine-year-old than gaining an extra day's holiday from school, especially a boarding school. I can still recall the joy of snuggling down in my own bed, knowing my chums would be tossing and turning in the first night misery of being back in the school dormitory.

Neither of my parents could escort me to school the following day, so arrangements were made for someone from school to meet me at Liverpool Street if I travelled to London alone. This I did: but on alighting from the train there was no one. I approached a policeman for help. As I was explaining my problem to him I heard above the hiss and clamour of Liverpool Street, 'Will Master David Ransom please go

to the Station Master's office.' 'Is that you?' said the bobby. 'Yes!' I replied fearfully, convinced that no good would come from such a summons, whereupon he took my hand, causing me to feel acutely exposed to censorious public gaze, and led me to the Station Master's office.

We were ushered immediately into the presence of the great man himself. 'Young man,' he said. 'Your headmaster has phoned me and asked me to put you in a taxi to the school. This policeman will find a taxi for you and explain your predicament to the driver.' And, of course, this is precisely what happened. What would a child do today, I wonder? Would a parent dare to put a nine-year-old child on a train alone? My second public address call was in circumstances all commuters dread. The day you lose your season ticket. Somehow, I knew the instant I awoke that morning that I had left my wallet on the train the day before. 'Nothing's been handed in here,' said the young man at Ipswich when I rushed to the station at the crack of dawn. 'I'll give you a ring if it is.' He took my office phone number.

I bought a ticket and got on the train with a heavy heart. As I trudged off the platform at Liverpool Street, convinced I would be spending the first few minutes, if not hours, at work phoning credit card companies and sorting out the mess my carelessness had created, I heard my name '...go to the Information Office'. My wallet had been found! So don't despair if your name is called, and as for the fear that everyone is looking at you, forget it. With the exception of the odd kindly policeman no one takes a blind bit of notice. The demise of the Station Master doesn't seem to matter either.

DAVID RANSOM

OFF THE WALL

LYRICAL BALDERDASH

AN *OBSERVER* journalist recently quoted a friend who told him that writing a novel is easy. You simply get up in the morning, climb three flights of stairs to your study, open the window and throw yourself out. That has been a great comfort to me. I have wanted to write a novel for a long time and now I know that my failure is not due to lack of talent or imagination, as I had supposed. It's just that I live in a bungalow.

I've only done this and that this morning. Time-consuming, boring, and when you stop there's nothing to show for it. But as I did it I found myself humming 'My Grandfather's Clock' and thought again about the words. Do you recall them? 'My grandfather's clock was too tall for the shelf so it stood ninety years on the floor.' Question: How tall was it? No one is suggesting that it was a grandfather clock – it was simply too tall for the shelf. It was probably about four feet high, five at the outside. Now, don't fidget; concentrate and listen to the next line. 'It was taller by half than the old man himself, though it weighed not a penny-piece more.' Question: How tall was his grandfather? A five-foot clock would be very heavy, so Question: How fat was his grandfather? No, don't go away. There's more.

'In watching its pendulum swing to and fro many hours he had spent as a boy.' Many hours? Question: How bright was his grandfather? And the clock is remarkable too. 'For it struck twenty-four when he entered at the door with a blooming and beautiful bride.' Question: How did his grandmother come to marry this short, fat imbecile? Of course she was blind, poor girl. It's

the only explanation. She is never mentioned again in the song although her husband lived to be ninety and she must have produced at least one child. I think, myself, that she miraculously recovered her sight and left on the same day with the man who came to repair the clock.

It's extraordinary what can be found if you examine some of our familiar songs more closely. What about 'Did you not hear my lady go down the garden singing? Blackbird and thrush were silent to hear the alleys ringing.' Have you ever counted the decibels it would take to make an alley ring? Blackbird and thrush were silent. I should damn well think they would be. They'd be gripping their perches for dear life and have their wings stuffed into their ears.

And what about that poor man stumbling about in the snow outside the palace of Good King Wenceslas gathering winter fuel? The king asks his page if he knows him and is told, 'Sire, he lives a good league hence underneath the mountain, close against the forest fence etc.' So what's he doing there? If he lives right against the forest fence one thing's for sure. He hasn't struggled for a league through all that snow just to gather fu–u–el. I think he's a spy, but almost certainly unemployed.

If I think of any other songs that would bear examination I'll wake you.

NAOMI SIM

OFF THE CUFF

THE ART OF CONVERSATION

IT IS A TRUTH universally acknowledged that the three best topics of conversation are sex, religion and politics. The last two are reliable promoters of general conversation, but a chat about sex is best conducted on a one-to-one basis. Now that the closet door is open, I ask my neighbour at dinner, if he appears to be handsome and intelligent, whether he is heterosexual or homosexual. Sadly, I have to report that I never get a straight answer, in either sense of the word. The clergy are particularly elusive on the subject. It was fascinating to realise the number of people who actually saw the hand of God behind the thunderbolt that struck York Minster after Bishop Jenkins denied the creed he wantonly intones each Sunday. I believe I am one of them. I have never, in honesty, been able to invoke that creed.

The decline of faith within the Church does not mean that the human race feels no need of religion. It has been forced, for lack of good leadership, to work out its own means of salvation. I regard that as no bad thing and it certainly increases the conversational interest of the subject.

Politics is an area that leaves me, to my regret, completely cold. It amuses

me to see how long I can take part in a debate before it is discovered that I have not the slightest idea what I am talking about. One can cover one's tracks most efficaciously by begging in enthralled tones: 'Do please explain exactly what you mean when you say that.'

A well-meaning woman felt that the inhabitants of the sleepy Sussex town where I live needed their wits sharpening. She decided to start a salon. Nothing could be simpler, she reckoned; she would ask half a dozen people round once a week, instruct them to talk brilliantly and that would be that. Her guests assembled with no such expectations. However, life is sometimes unexpected. While our hostess was out of the room preparing the inevitable coffee and biscuits, her guests, they knew not how, found themselves deep in a discussion on the pros and cons of lesbianism, a diversion none of them had yet practised, although one was of the opinion that you should try everything once. Points of view were being sparked with commendable animation – until our hostess re-entered with the coffee-tray. When she heard the variety of the views expressed she very nearly dropped it. 'This,' she informed us, 'is the most disgusting subject. You are to stop it at once and talk of something wholesome.' As far as I remember we talked of the weather for half an hour and then went home.

> *Her guests, they knew not how, found themselves deep in a discussion on the pros and cons of lesbianism*

My strip of Sussex remains completely uncultured and unaware. One of the yeomen announced that of course he had voted Conservative. What was the point of taxing the rich so that they would not be able to employ the poor?

Another facet of the political scene: the eldest sons of those who shape our destinies invariably find their parents' fame a crippling burden. Robert Cecil was the younger son of Lord Burghley; William Pitt the younger son of Lord Chatham. Even they paid a price, being, from first to last, lonely men.

URSULA WYNDHAM

'Miss Benson, send in a scapegoat'

WORLD'S
WORST
DUMPS

Monaco

The only thing missing is the tumbleweed, says **EDMUND DULAC**

Monaco is the Mediterranean's answer to Singapore. What must have been once a pleasant and rather special spot is now nothing but tower blocks and civic discipline. It is also the only place in the world where I have been thrown out of a restaurant for ordering a meal that was insufficiently expensive.

If you are not paying attention you might well travel right through Monaco without realising that you have ever left France, but if you break your drowse in the passenger seat or actually get off the train, you'll soon enough discover that the Principality is strangely clean and strangely empty.

It is clean because a discreet army of proles creeps about in the shrubberies pouncing on cigarette ends. At the end of the working day these persons evaporate into the velvet air not to reappear until dawn. The boast is that you can eat your breakfast off the pavements, and you could perhaps do so provided only that a) you were

> **There are, apparently, 128,000 bank accounts in Monaco, but there are no people. Well, only a few**

in possession of the price of a Monaco breakfast (not always easy in a tax haven where evidence that you are worth US $1,000,000 is a prerequisite for a residence permit) and b) that you are not caught by the local police.

These latter, the self-consciously mustachioed public face of a Ruritanian police state, wear spats and white helmets modelled on those of the British bobby. Their weapon is the whistle. Stop the car for a micro-second in the wrong place and PEEP you are being waved imperiously on; step over the low chain that separates the parade ground of the miniature palace from the public street and PEEP you are being ordered off.

Shame, and a faint sense that you are on alien territory – Mars-on-Sea as it were – makes you react to this whistling with Pavlovian promptitude.

Clean, and strangely empty. In the summer the tourists drive through. The Italians come in coach-loads and, absurdly, look at the cathedral, which bears to the great churches of Italy the same sort of relation that Wigan Comprehensive bears to Winchester.

The millionaires park their yachts next to one another in the harbour and buy flats as a tax break. The names on the sterns give away the strange, microscopic, uprooted world in which these people live: *Jason II* or *Evening Star III*, you read, and underneath Isle of Man or Jersey or Bahamas – on these boats you manage to be offshore twice in one go. But the millionaires are not there of course – the yachts sit empty and the flats reveal their merely fiscal status by showing, as evening sets in, no lights. There are, apparently, 128,000 bank accounts in Monaco, but there are no people.

Well, only a few. The Glitterati emerge at certain times and in certain places to complain about their alcohol problems and their boredom. A thirtysomething Anglo couple I met, when asked what they did in Monaco, answered, 'We are practising otiosity.' Laziness by any other name is just as dull. Besides eating-breakfast-off-the-pavement, the other cliché of the place is that you can walk down the streets at 3 am, alone, wearing a diamond necklace, in complete safety. It's probably true. The surveillance cameras and the Carry-on-in-Ruritania policemen are keeping watch.

I have never entirely subscribed to the anti-antiseptic, muck-and-bullets school of thought (you know, Give Me a Provençal Peasant Over a Sanitised Swede Any Day) but in Monaco you can find yourself yearning for the Gorbals. Even Switzerland is more fun.

The night belongs to Nell

NELL DUNN, *no stranger to the darkest hour, considers the twilight world of the insomniac*

I USED TO FEAR sleepless nights. When I lay awake in the small hours, my thoughts would be of the next day and of how exhausted I would be and a panic would settle in me. My body would ache and a sensation of despair creep through my heart and settle in my mind. Indeed I would wake exhausted and depressed, and driven to all the small businesses of the next day would find no pleasure, no pleasure at all in being alive.

However, since becoming an oldie, all this has changed. Sometimes I sleep alone, sometimes with my best friend. If I wake when he is there I lie and listen to his breathing and feel pleased that we are still together and alive. I even feel quite cheerful. Then I usually fall asleep.

If I am alone I have a more unpredictable time. I've got a bed I like and a very light goose-down duvet and a really comfy pillow. I have a good radio – not a battery one as they kept running out – but a plug-in one with several buttons for easy search of different stations. I've also got a bottle of mineral water and a favourite Georges Simenon, a writer who is such an ace at understanding night and aloneness, as did Graham Greene. I listened to Julian Glover reading *The End of the Affair* on the World Service the other night. What a writer, what a book. I lay there in my lovely bed, the room gently lit by the street lights shining through the blinds,

listening to that marvellous passage where the bomb drops and the door falls on him and he frees himself and goes back into the bedroom to find his mistress naked and praying by the bed and when she sees him:

> *She turned quickly and stared at me with fear. I hadn't realised that my dressing gown was torn and dusted all over with plaster; my hair was white with it and there was blood on my mouth and cheeks. 'Oh, God,' she said, 'you're alive.'*

Sometimes I go downstairs to the kitchen and make myself a cup of tea and then the dogs wake and want to come up to bed with me and I usually let them and we all snuggle up together. Jack Russells lie extraordinarily still in the night, although Ivy has a slight

> *I used to fear sleepless nights. I would wake exhausted and depressed. Since becoming an oldie all this has changed*

snore from a damaged larynx sustained as a puppy when she was dragged along by her lead being accidentally trapped in the car door.

By now I feel close to myself and warm and ready to drift off. Other times I fancy a bit of telly. There is often a film on at about 2.30 am. It's *Chinatown* this Friday and I hope I wake up. Sometimes I do feel tired the next day but it is often the kind of tiredness I felt as a young woman when I had stayed up all night at a party or in a lover's arms – an exhilarated tiredness, the tiredness of time well spent, of having stolen a march on the sleeping population.

A SCHOLAR and a GENTLEMAN

Energetic, eccentric, frugal and generous,
JOCK MURRAY *was a bookman of the old school,*
the sixth of his line. **DERVLA MURPHY** *recalls her*
long-standing friendship with the bibliophile, Byron-
lover and inspired editor who published her first book

My last letter to my publisher, written from South Africa a few weeks before his death, told the sort of true traveller's tale that delighted John Murray VI. Arriving at sunset in the isolated hamlet of Campbell on the edge of the Great Karoo, I had some difficulty finding lodgings; the local Afrikaners spoke no English and were suspicious of a female sexagenarian bicyclist, suddenly appearing out of nowhere. Then, in a tiny stone church built by English missionaries in 1832, I noticed a dusty glass-topped display case containing Livingstone's *Missionary Travels in South Africa* (1857). This large volume, open at the title page, gave the publisher's name and address: John Murray, 50 Albemarle Street, London. One hundred and thirty-six years later another Murray author drew from her passport that letter (To Whom It May Concern) with which Jock thoughtfully equipped 'his' travellers at the beginning of each journey. It was headed John Murray, 50 Albemarle Street, London. Beckoning to the uneasy Afrikaner couple now dwelling in Livingstone's Campbell home, I pointed to the title page and then to my letter. At once they relaxed and smiled and invited me to stay the night. Even in the Karoo, pampered Murray authors can have occasion to feel grateful.

Jock's relish for such linkages, and his lifelong obsession with the late Lord Byron, did not prevent his seeing in which direction Murrays should turn during the post-war years – a critical period for publishers. He marvellously combined the romantic – revering the past and to an extent emotionally dependent on it – with the shrewd businessman who realised that a successful publisher must have one foot in the future. The witty social Jock, all bonhomie and graciousness, eschewing the vulgarity of money talk, knew how to keep his own distinctive show on the road in defiance of transnational highwaymen. The House of Murray has survived since 1768 because each generation had the vision to adapt without compromising standards. The weight of tradition, although formidable indeed by the time Jock joined the firm in 1930, was never allowed to smother innovation.

But for a chance encounter with Penelope Betjeman I would never have met Jock Murray. Having cycled to India in 1963 I met her in Delhi and as we pedalled together through a crowded bazaar – Penelope with a load of firewood tied perilously to her carrier – I confessed to literary ambitions.

'Of course!' shrieked Penelope. 'Marvellous journey! Marvellous book! You must send it to Jock Murray.'

'To whom?' I yelled above the blare of rickshaw horns. 'To Jock Murray in Albemarle Street. You'll *adore* Jock. Everybody adores Jock!'

This suggestion genuinely shocked me; *lèse-majesté* and all that. John Murray was associated in my mind with Jane Austen, Byron, Borrow, Darwin, Livingstone, Isabella Bird, Younghusband – not to mention Freya Stark, at whose shrine I had been worshipping since early childhood when *The Valley of the Assassins* was read to me by my mother.

Back in Ireland, I ignored Penelope's preposterous advice and simultaneously sent off three copies of the *Full Tilt* typescript, not really expecting anyone to accept it. Embarrassingly, everyone accepted it. Hastening to London to deal with this contretemps, I didn't like what I found. Not for nothing was I a county librarian's daughter who by the age of ten could tell from a distance the publisher of a given volume. (Fifty years ago imprints maintained a decent consistency.) I went on to develop some awareness of publishers' wily ways and in London I sensed heavy editorial hands all poised to turn *my* book into *their* book. ('Perhaps we could expand a little on that attempted rape…') Telling everyone I would think about their offer I returned home and found a letter from Penelope – 'Have you sent your book to Jock Murray? If not, why not?' Thus it happened that a faint and dog-eared carbon copy went off to No. 50 Albemarle Street.

A week later I had been summoned to The Presence by telegram and was ascending that hallowed staircase, quite unwomanned by suspense and awe. Jock's office was cramped, chaotic and almost as dusty as my own house. Typescripts, photographs, maps, manuscripts, newspaper cuttings, dust-jackets, bulging files and books old and new cluttered every surface, including the floor. In a corner sat 'young John', as he was then known, experiencing his first week as a publisher and looking almost as nervous as I felt. (Now that neophyte is John VII – which, it suddenly strikes me, has a disconcertingly papal ring.) This was a reassuring scene, far removed from the bright, tidy, sterile offices of Those Others. Very soon I no longer felt nervous. The legendary Jock alchemy was working; it seemed I had known this adorable person (Penelope had been right!) not for minutes but for years. Jock wanted to publish my *Full Tilt* and there was no squalid talk about baffling royalty percentages and terrifying promotion campaigns. Then came an invitation to stay at Cannon Lodge; like many another Murray author, I had found not only a publisher but a whole family of friends.

The legendary Jock alchemy was working; it seemed I had known this adorable person not for minutes but for years

Jock was an exhilarating mix of the conventional and the eccentric. Stacking plates was an unforgivable crime but driving through red traffic lights – given a sporting chance of getting away with it – was just good fun. (Good fun for Jock, not necessarily for his passengers.) His famous frugality – typified by turning off lights in unoccupied rooms, wearing a slight frown as a general reprimand to whomever might have left them on – exactly accorded with my own. It could however slightly irritate some of the younger generation who found it difficult to reconcile with his equally famous generosity, overlooking the simple mathematical fact that the frugal have more with which to be generous.

Frugality also determined Jock's advances to authors. He rightly expected a book to prove its worth before its publisher disbursed. The headline-grabbing advances with which the more notorious conglomerates wage their sordid wars caused Jock to smile one of his rather wicked small smiles and say nothing. Now, while those conglomerates lurch from crisis to crisis in a stormy sea of their own creation, loaded with bewildered, seasick authors, the little House of Murray sails serenely on.

Many of the Murrays' 'extended family' of author-friends who enjoyed the hospitality of Cannon Lodge will remember Jock's disingenuous habit of suggesting that 'early beds' would be a good idea. Then, having genially but firmly shepherded everyone upstairs, he would sneak away to work for two or three midnight hours on some typescript in urgent need of loving editorial care. And loving care was what those typescripts got, down to the last dash (of which he disapproved, *pace* Byron) and semi-colon. As an editorial team, he and his wife Diana were inspired and inspiring. Jock's several pages of notes in tiny handwriting ('mere minutiae' he would murmur self-deprecatingly) acted like those pinches of yeast that lighten a mass of dough. Then Diana would produce her notes, approaching the typescript's problems from quite other but equally important angles; this was yin and yang in perfect balance. The loving care devoted to typescripts was extended to their creators, whether successful or not. So tender-hearted was Jock that even unknown would-be authors caused him many a sleepless night. How to word a kind rejection letter to someone who had plainly laboured for years on some utterly unpublishable work? Regularly Jock was reminded that printed rejection slips are standard practice in the modern age; then he would brandish his eyebrows in his inimitable way, thus conveying that no such barbarism was acceptable to him.

At the root of Jock's celebrated charm was his respect for his fellow beings and his awareness of their vulnerability. The effervescent, inquisitive, enthusiastic Jock, often melodramatically gesturing, usually ready with the appropriate aphorism or *bon mot*, was in part a cover-up for that other Jock whose own vulnerability was extreme and whose last months were darkened by the Bosnian tragedy. His caring for his authors was only one aspect of his caring for all of humanity.

Banged UP

Treading a fine line: a night in the cells, by **NICKY BIRD**

It was not how I intended to spend Tuesday night. The cell was not cramped, as cells go, but as cells go it lacked the homely touch. Sitting on the blue plastic mattress I mentally decorated the room. For a start the lavatory would have to go from its position in front of the door. Call me old-fashioned, but I prefer a more secluded spot, away from the peep-hole. And I do think a lavatory-seat a delightful accessory, silly softy that I am. Chipped enamel is so abrasive. When the nice policeman eventually let me out I asked him why they dispensed with this modest luxury. 'Suicide,' he muttered. When I worked in Toilet Requisites at Barkers I never realised I was selling a lethal weapon.

The lighting was atrocious, nothing could be done with the proportions of the room and the faecal brown colour-scheme cried out for decorative relief; thankfully a man signing himself 'Knobhead' had drawn a dramatic scene featuring Adam and Eve and the improper use of a police truncheon.

I have been arrested, mostly for minor offences, several times. The first was in France for hitting a gendarme with a snowball. It was a good shot and I didn't regret the instant fine or the sobering hour inside the almost chic cell. The following winter I was allowed to compare cells. *Nul points* for Britain. But our bobby was top of the league. He called me 'sir', brought me tea, and hoped my stay had been an agreeable one.

When confronted with an aggressive copper there are two types of middle-class reaction: outrage or servility

It is all very different now. Years of yobbery and violence have made the police understandably nervous of even cut-price offenders like myself. When confronted with an aggressive copper there are two types of middle-class reaction: pompous outrage or cringing servility, which is my favoured method. But it doesn't stop you being treated like a potential serial killer. I couldn't be more pleasant and co-operative. I laugh at their jokes about black men, share my sweeties, and even claim that many of my best friends are Masons. But I am still barked at: 'Keep your hands on the fucking table!' Then it's, 'Get in there!' and I walk meekly into the cell and I wait.

And wait. It is clear I have been forgotten. Without a watch, I only roughly compute the time it takes to read several stanzas of graffiti and a bus ticket fifty times, exercise my knee, stare through the perspex peep-hole at the coppers and contemplate my down-ward mobility. Hours.

An Acton accountant was arrested the other day at dawn for the most footling offence. A weedy, harmless fellow, he had his hands handcuffed behind his back for all his neighbours to see. Take from him his reputation and respectability and he is lost. By great good fortune, as a hack and househusband I have none to lose.

With my one phone call I rang the wife but got the answering-machine. No one knows I'm here. I pictured her annoyance when she eventually discovered I had been incarcerated and hadn't vamoosed with a floozie. The fine would be unpopular. Failure to pass a breath-test is expensive.

I started to bang quietly on the door, a delicate operation designed to attract attention without giving offence or an impression I had gone berserk. An eye appeared at the peep-hole. I saw a policeman stroll to the desk and mouth, 'There's someone in there, Sarge'. 'Fuck me.' The Sergeant wandered over and let me out.

'We were rather busy,' he lied. Reverting to my cringing mood I thanked him for his hospitality and the use of his comfy bed but he mistook grovelling for sarcasm. I could see he was turning nasty. 'You can go,' he growled. I toddled off home.

'See you soon!' he shouted after me, recognising a recidivist when he saw one.

JOHN WATSON

TOP CHUMPS

TOM CRUISE

CHUMPFILE ▶

★ Admired by Jonathan Ross	95%
★ Real name Mapother IV	100%
★ Jumping on Oprah couch	100%
★ Scientology nut	100%
★ Friend of Xenu	93%
★ Cuban heels	92%

Miles Kington

The psychology of the waiting game

Last Thursday I discovered a good place for a psychiatrist to be. It was in the queue at the fish stall at Bradford-on-Avon market. When it was my turn, an elderly lady who had been behind me in the queue suddenly metamorphosed into the woman in front of me and proceeded to start buying her fish.

'I think I was first,' I said.

She looked at me as if I had made an obscene suggestion.

'No,' she said, 'I was here...' and she vaguely motioned towards her feet. Only the lingering suspicion that maybe, just maybe, I was mistaken restrained me from making a scene. What I really wanted to do was take her by the throat and shake her, shouting: 'All my life I have been plagued by little old ladies like you, who blatantly and ruthlessly queue-barge, and go ahead of law-abiding people like me, and it is only the thought that you have less time left on this earth than I have that makes me let you get away with it!'

If there had been a psychiatrist standing by, he could either have talked me out of a murder attempt or started a study of the murderous habit of old ladies in queues. It's true. All classes of society do their share of queue-jumping but in my experience old women are by far the worst. They leap for an opening like a rugby three-quarter going for the try line. They have techniques for doing it, too, like pretending to look at prices, or wanting to look at the produce at the far end of the counter and never returning...

'You were right,' said the old man behind me in the queue when she had gone. You were first. She was cutting in.'

When somebody writes a work on the psychology of queuing there must a chapter on ruthless old ladies. But the day after the fish stall experience I discovered a whole new field for a queue psychologist. It was at Heathrow Airport, Terminal 4, where I was waiting at Arrivals for Canadian in-laws to come tumbling out. It took an hour for them to appear, during which time I was deeply absorbed by watching the manner in which people greet each other.

> ## What I really wanted to do was take her by the throat and shake her, shouting

Of course, a lot of people there had not come to do any greeting, only to do some picking up and chauffeuring. They were the dark-suited ones with hand-written placards reading 'Mr Wallington' or 'Blakeney Cars', very few of whom ever seemed to meet their intended customer.

But most of the waiters were relatives and loved ones who

'Isn't she something in MI5?'

finally saw their target come out of the hidden customs area and either rushed forward to greet them or waved, shouting: 'Hello! Hello!' And when the final impact came, I observed something I had never observed before: that in any embrace one party to the embrace is less enthusiastic about it than the other one. When mothers hug spotty teenagers, the teenager is embarrassed while the mother is ecstatic. When hosts greet incoming visitors, the visitor tends to hang back. When loved ones meet, one of them is gladder to see the other than the other is, and one of them is more keen to tell the other what a terrible journey/ wait/drive to the airport they had.

Even techniques vary. When one side comes forward to deliver a kiss on the cheek or a handshake, and the other side is prepared for a hug, there is a moment of complete emotional turmoil, and even some physical damage. And I'll tell you something else. When you have been waiting for a whole hour, and no Canadian in-law has appeared, you get desperate for *someone* to embrace. You can feel this welcome building up inside you, and you know it will go to waste if it isn't used soon... That's why, when a rather handsome woman appeared and was perfunctorily hugged by some stranger, I stepped forward and tapped him on the shoulder.

'Excuse me,' I said, 'I think I was first in the queue.'

And I gave the astonished woman a smacking kiss and a far warmer hug than the man had managed. She was not, I think, ungrateful, even if the presence of the man forced her to pretend to be indignant...

The GNOME SPOTTER

It was not until he reached middle age that **JOHN McEWEN** *realised how much of his surviving sense of wonder he owed to 'BB', author of 'The Little Grey Men'*

'B B' was the pseudonym of the author and artist Denys Watkins-Pitchford. His favourite sport was wildfowling and 'BB' was the tradename of the heaviest goose-shot cartridges. 'BB' was born on 25th July 1905 and died on 8th September 1990. He was always grateful for the luck to be born when he was: 'A few years earlier and I'd have been killed as a subaltern on the Western Front.' His writing career began in 1939 with publication of the story of a fox, *Wild Lone*, illustrated – as all his books would be – by himself under his proper name, D J Watkins-Pitchford. His most famous was *The Little Grey Men*, a children's adventure story about some gnomes who went in search of their long-lost brother. It was inspired by his own incontrovertible sighting of a gnome at the age of four. He was a down-to-earth man and never budged on this issue; though latterly he felt that gnomes, like so much of the countryside, might have become extinct during his lifetime.

The Little Grey Men won the Carnegie Prize, encouraging him to give up his first and only job as assistant art master at Rugby. 'BB' published over sixty books plus a great deal of journalism, much of it as a columnist for the *Shooting Times*. He was most popular in the 1940s and 1950s. *Brendon Chase*,

his own favourite from among his books, was published in 1944. It drew on his experience at Rugby and told the tale of three boys who run away from boarding school to live by their

> **The book was inspired by his own incontrovertible sighting of a gnome at the age of four**

wits in an English forest. Its success could be gauged, to his amusement, by the number of irate letters from headmasters cursing him for yet another break-out. Certainly it was a bible to countless country-bred prep and public schoolboys.

I write as a *Brendon Chase* addict who had the good fortune to become a friend of the author. As a commissioning editor on *The Field*

under Simon Courtauld in the mid-1980s I discovered that 'BB' was still alive and writing. Shamefully I had long consigned him to oblivion. First the film-star 'BB' had supplanted him in my affections, and then London. Now it dawned on me in middle age that it was to him I owed most of the little wonder I retained. I fired off a passionate letter of thanks.

I anticipated his reply with the impatience of a schoolboy awaiting a love letter. It eventually arrived, typed and signed with both his names. 'I am just emerging from a dark valley having had an operation for prostate in the local hospital, a period of anxiety and discomfort which I hope will soon be forgotten. I am in my eightieth year, blind in my right eye, but feeling as young and eager as ever I did. What a pity the envelope which encloses us wears out so soon!'

This was to be a recurring pattern and refrain. Ill-health dogged him until the end, though not for one

Left: 'BB' in the garden of the Round House. 'BB's scraperboard illustrations from *The Little Grey Men – facing page*: headpiece from the Contents page (far left); 'Baldmoney' (centre); 'Robin' headpiece from 'The Jeannie Deans' chapter (bottom). *This page*: headpiece from the Introduction (left); 'Dodder weeps' (bottom)

twin brother Roger. His wife had died twenty years before, poisoned – he was convinced – by inhaling wind-blown insecticide. On the mantelpiece was an early 1950s snapshot of him with his son Robin, aged eight, both with guns. Robin had died shortly after it was taken of a painful and mysterious illness, the bitterest of blows.

'BB's own childhood had been spent entirely at home because of ill-health, which did not prevent him hunting with gun, rod or butterfly-net, on horseback or on foot, to his heart's content. This bred in him a reverence for the chase he never lost – from ignorance of it townspeople were for him 'only half alive' – and an attendant and instinctive knowledge and love of nature. No one has drawn or painted Northamptonshire's landscape better, its shaggy hedges and ivy-muffled trees; or brought such 'moonlight witchery', as a New York reviewer called it, to scraperboard illustration. And his always poetic descriptions have an animal keenness of perception, sounds and smells as sharply evoked as any sight. He wrote when the mood took him and with an undiminished spontaneity. Even from hospital he regaled readers of the *Shooting Times* with his sighting of a duck-shaped cloud, the manoeuvres of ants on his window-sill and the comforting companionship of a 'tall douglas fir, with its dark gloomy interior'.

It was no surprise to learn that readers would write or visit at the rate of at least one a week to thank him for saving them from suicide; that one thousand carp fishers, a fraternity created by his *Confessions of a Carp Fisher*, rose as one to acclaim him at a surprise dinner; that he was the favourite author of Richard Walker, most legendary of post-war fishermen, Ranulph Fiennes and Julie Andrews. This only hints at the great love so many of us had and have for him, last of the old poet naturalists.

PHOTOGRAPH COURTESY © NORTHAMPTONSHIRE NEWSPAPERS

second did he fail to live by the old and anonymous valediction with which he prefaced all his books: 'The wonder of the world, the beauty and the power, the shapes of things, their colours, lights and shades; these I saw. Look ye also while life lasts.'

The day came when I, like many before me, made the pilgrimage to Sudborough in Northamptonshire. He was a short man, with an old-fashioned moustache, notably flat ears and the tinge of a Northamptonshire accent in his deep voice, which often broke into a gruff laugh. The initials of 'Bill Badger', a later character of his, coincidentally matched his pseudonym. Badgers are always warriors in his books – significantly, the 'Bill Badger' series was particularly successful in Japan – and 'BB' was a warrior. He spoke with gusto of his time as a Special Constable in the General Strike, knocking sense into the skulls of Camden Town hooligans. And he had a badgerish taste for 'dens'.

'BB' lived in an old and conical gatehouse in Sudborough. The Round House was instantly recognisable as his abode by its weathervane – a wild goose of his own design. There he lived with his daughter Angela and

ANGUS AND JANE

OTHER PEOPLE: *a portrait portfolio of the modern types you meet, but perhaps rather wouldn't*

Angus and Jane are married, just. Since the Maida Vale flat was sold, Angus has skulked in his Gloucestershire cottage, while Jane has bought a smaller flat near the bookshop where she works. Occasionally they speak on the telephone. More frequently, they speak to each other's answering machines.

When Angus and Jane married four years ago, their friends were delighted but surprised. Jane's first husband had been a powerful, charismatic man, possessed of narcissistic good looks and the morals of a virus. Fatally addicted to cliché, he had succumbed to an unusually acute mid-life crisis in his forties and run off with his secretary.

Angus, by almost comic contrast, was short and rotund, always laughing, a bit of a character. Long widowed, he had survived 35 years in advertising by being a bit of a character, by always laughing, and by manipulating and manoeuvring behind the scenes with unsqueamish ruthlessness. Jane found the combination intriguing, and was willing to overlook his less appealing physical attributes. She had been mourning the loss of her husband – last heard of in Los Angeles with his latest pregnant twenty-five-year-old Nigerian girlfriend – for too long. Angus was good company. And after three decades at the top of his profession, he was rich enough to keep her in a style to which she looked forward to becoming accustomed. Jane was bored with genteel poverty. She still had her St John's Wood flat, the last remaining prize of her divorce settlement, but even that would have to go soon.

'But why don't you just live with him?' trilled her daughters, when she told them that Angus had proposed. Jane could see the logic of their argument, and had no strong moral objection to the idea – both her daughters lived with their boyfriends, and she had never worried about that. But like Elizabeth Taylor, she had long since decided that she was the marrying kind. They put their flats on the market, and prepared for married life.

> **Jane cannot remember when she first began to entertain doubts, though the three-day honeymoon may have been a clue**

Jane cannot remember when she first began to entertain doubts, although she now realises that the three-day honeymoon may have been a clue. Immediately after their return, Angus flew on to Hong Kong on an urgent business trip. Jane supervised the transfer of her own and Angus's belongings to the new flat. Several beloved artefacts failed to survive the move. Her cat, angry at the disturbance, urinated over Angus's favourite armchair. These were stressful weeks for Jane. Out in Hong Kong, Angus's urgent business trip continued apparently indefinitely, all expenses paid.

When Angus finally returned, Jane found him less jolly and entertaining than of old. In public he remained the life and soul. At home he was morose and pedantic. At first their differences were trivial. He liked his tea brewed in a mug, to the strength and consistency of bitumen. She preferred a pot of Earl Grey. He objected to the smell of her cat's litter. She wished he would wash his handkerchiefs more often. And so on.

But more fundamental disagreements threatened. Angus now spent most of his days at home. Neither his various consultancies nor his chairmanship of an up-and-coming agency seemed to stretch him terribly hard. Even so, he still expected Jane to cook him dinner every night. Tired after a long day at the bookshop, Jane watched as Angus shovelled the fruits of her culinary skills into his gaping maw. At night, as she lay in bed, she could still hear his furious chewing, and see in her mind's eye flecks of mashed potato splashed across his fleshy lips.

The sex was unfortunate. Perhaps physical

attraction would have made a difference after all. Angus's changes of mood were becoming increasingly unpredictable. When Jane bought herself a new coat he trudged gloomily around the flat as though a close relative had died. Relations between Angus and the cat declined. The cat spat whenever she saw him. Angus said she was 'vermin'. The cat urinated in one of his shoes.

Jane was noticing more and more about Angus, and liking less and less. Whenever he came home he wiped his shoes not on the mat outside but on her Chinese rug inside. When he washed up, which wasn't often, he never washed the lids of the saucepans, so that they gradually accumulated layers of grime that Jane found impossible to remove. He was a hypochondriac, who became convinced that he had caught shingles from an insect bite, despite no physical evidence of shingles or, indeed, an insect bite.

Worst of all, he was a tightwad. Absurdly generous during their courtship, Angus now seemed determined to hang on to every penny. Before they married, they had agreed that each would be responsible for his or her own immediate expenses, and that Angus would cover the housekeeping. His income, though infinitely mysterious, was known to be by far the greater. Three months after the wedding, Angus proposed that Jane should pay half of the housekeeping in the future, as she was rich, and he was finding it hard to make ends meet.

Ah, so that was it, thought Jane. He's after my money. What a shame I haven't got any. Meanwhile Angus was warming to his theme. Why did they need a cleaning woman? Why did Jane bother to work at all? She didn't need the money. He would much prefer to have Jane at home with him all day, cooking all his meals, tending to all his needs...

A week later Jane ejected Angus from the marital bed. The cat developed severe bruising on her lower abdomen, and hid whenever Angus was in the room. Angus spent every weekend in Gloucestershire, either alone or with his grown-up children. Jane heard a rumour that he had signed over most of his assets to them in the event of a divorce settlement.

Fortunately their lawyers get on famously.

MARCUS BERKMANN

The great actor always had impeccable timing, says **JOHN WELLS**

Sir Laurence Olivier

THE LATE SIR Laurence Olivier exercised an eerie fascination over me from the first time I ever saw him act in the film version of *Hamlet*. It was something to do with the way he arranged his face before he spoke, and then pushed the familiar English language about into weird shapes, rather in the way Gerald Scarfe distorts the human face.

It was still recognisable as English, but the pleasure was not so much in listening to the meaning as to the funny cadences, the unexpected swoops, mutters and yelps.

It was a style that achieved its fullest flowering in his Richard III, where the distortions in the language were echoed by the cartoon figure on the screen, the hump, the nose and the funny walk.

I first saw him in the flesh, without really meeting him, in Sean Kenny's office in Greek Street some time in 1964, when he came in to talk about the set for a play Sean was designing. Sean was a small, tough, broadshouldered Irishman, who could lift a car onto the pavement if he didn't like the way it was parked, and frequently hit people, and I was alarmed when Sir Laurence laid a languid arm round his shoulders, rolled his eyes and said, 'Hello, Shawnie Baby!'

Sean didn't hit him, but I was surprised how concerned Olivier was about timing and delivery, even off stage.

I am not sure whether that mystery was solved about five years after that, when I met him. I had translated Danton's *Death* for the National Theatre. The play was directed by Jonathan Miller, and Christopher Plummer was playing Danton.

Shortly before the dress rehearsal there was some disagreement or other. Christopher Plummer was brooding in his dressing room, and

Laurence Olivier as Richard III

Olivier, the director of the National Theatre, came down to the theatre to smooth things over. Jonathan Miller had encouraged the designers to eschew the obvious, and apart from some glass cases containing dresses, the only scenery consisted of two plaster figures accurately modelled on the male anatomy – with the skin or muscles peeled back here and there to demonstrate the working parts – standing left and right on either side of the forestage.

Both were, I think, modelled from life, one with ampler external organs than the other. It was to this one that Sir Laurence seemed drawn, and we ambled across the stage to examine it.

After a while he asked Jonathan in the familiar cracked articulation: 'Tell me, Jon-ath-an, sum-thing I have nevah un-der-stood: how does the bludd get into the pee-nis to create an e-rec-shun?'

Jonathan fluttered his hands and explained with his characteristic hurried hesitancy that 'it wasn't so much the blood getting into the penis, it was more a kind of brake operation that prevented it from getting out.'

Sir Laurence pondered this in silence for a moment or two, and then said with the familiar upward inflection, '*Ejaculatio praecox*... The story of my life!'

Esprit de GORE

This article by **CAROLINE RICHMOND** *is about people who perform operations on themselves. It's undoubtedly the most bloodcurdling thing we've ever published. You have been warned...*

Illustrations by JON CRAMER

Tired of waiting for your operation? Can't get a surgeon to do exactly what you want? Disappointed that you can't have your op performed by the theatre nurse? You could try doing it yourself. Plenty of other people have done so. Sometimes this has been an urgent matter. For example my friend Vic the former squadron leader used black Sylko to repair a gash in his leg after a bullet wound. There was, he said, no one else around, so he just got on with it. So did a retired major in Sussex: after I wrote about self-surgery in a doctors' magazine I received a letter from Dr Stanley Surtees at Eastbourne General Hospital, who wrote: 'Some twenty years ago I had a patient (a sixty-year-old male) who self-amputated his leg at the knee joint. He sat in the

bath and did it with a razor blade and when admitted with some shock he was otherwise remarkably well. With a suitable prosthesis he lived for another seven or eight years, although I am glad to say he moved to Cornwall. I don't think he was a diagnosably psychiatric patient but just a very precise ex-serviceman who decided on this line of action to prove something to himself.'

Toes were the abiding interest of Mr A, a New Yorker who, by the age of seventy-two, had been pulling out his toenails for over fifty years. In the early 1930s he worked as a farrier, shoeing horses for the US cavalry, and his feet were often injured in the line of duty, causing infections and ingrowing toe-nails. Perhaps deciding that what was sauce for the horse was sauce for him, he pulled out his nails with pliers, and has done so ever since. By the age of sixty he had destroyed so many nerves

that the procedure had become completely painless; also, as the years went by his nails became smaller and grew more slowly. He would soften the nails with petrolatum and then pull out the two sets on consecutive days, covering his nail beds with antibiotic ointment and wrapping them in gauze.

But the real stars of the world of self-surgery are people who have, er, wanted something a little, er, special. Most of them wanted their gonads removed. Most of them are men.

The first recorded case was in 1882. The American *Journal of Insanity* reported that a thirty-seven-year-old man circumcised himself and, not content with that, cut himself open from pubic bone to navel to see what was inside him. After some stitches and a stay in hospital he went home 'completely cured', only to return a year later with his scrotum slit open and his testicles dropping out. More stitches, and nine days in hospital followed. Another year passed, and he popped in to have his second abdominal opening sewn up. Shortly afterwards he performed a 'regular castration' of one testicle, suturing his scrotum carefully. As soon as the wound healed he did the other side but this time the ligature he had tied around his spermatic cord slipped off and he bled profusely. Nevertheless, he recovered completely with a bit of help from the hospital.

According to Dr John Money of the Johns Hopkins Medical School in Maryland, people do it to change sex or become totally celibate. When, in 1979, Johns Hopkins held a press conference announcing that they were banning sex-change operations, one disappointed punter blasted

his genitalia off with a gun. Mr G, a New Yorker, excised his scrotum and testicles with a kitchen knife while immersed in the ocean because he thought the cool water would act as an anaesthetic. This was no impulse; he had previously asked a surgeon to remove them. He returned home and handed his testicles to his mother, who flushed them down the lavatory.

Doctors like to collect case reports that have a common theme, no matter how recondite, and surgeons Jeremy Thompson and T K Abraham at Ealing Hospital collected two cases of men who chopped themselves after the death of their fathers. Mr E, a young van driver, tried to circumcise himself 'because he thought it might lift him out of his depression' three days after the bereavement. Mr F, a single man, was admitted as an emergency after removing his left testicle and half his right one in deference to his late father. He allowed his wounds to be sewed up but refused a blood transfusion 'as an insupportable invasion of his privacy'. In a previous incarnation, he said, he had led a large religious movement in eighteenth-century Russia, was persecuted, and had castrated himself with a red-hot poker. A psychiatrist found him lucid and rational, and he was discharged home where he killed himself with weedkiller.

But the most famous of all was a gifted student obsessed with celibacy. At twenty-one he lost his virginity to a woman who complained that he was a bad lover, who kissed too hard and banged into her too hard, so he asked a surgeon to castrate him to treat his 'excessive aggressiveness'; he wanted a 'hugging and kissing' relationship with a woman. On being refused castration, he had started frequenting the medical

faculty library and treating himself. First he dosed himself with female hormones to decrease his male hormones. This, he said, was a time of well-being. Then he decided to immunise himself against his own hormones, a procedure that had been tried experimentally in farm animals but not in humans. He injected a sophisticated mixture of hormones and immunology reagents into his legs but these caused abscesses. Next he tried visiting nearby cities, seeking physicians who would help him with hormone treatments. After four months of this he carefully castrated himself, and got his local hospital to check his handiwork and close the wound. Then, alas, he read that he would still be producing male hormone from his adrenal glands, and that these might have stepped up production after his castration. This could be prevented by cutting the nerve supply to the glands.

At four o'clock on the morning of his surgery he disinfected his bedsitter with spray disinfectant and draped an area with sheets that he had sterilised the

day before. He took barbiturate tablets to partly anaesthetise himself, and hydrocortisone to combat stress. In case of surgical shock, he prepared a spray can of adrenalin. Wearing sterile gloves and a surgical mask, he lay supine and worked via strategically placed mirrors. He swabbed his abdomen with alcohol, made an incision with a scalpel, and used retractors to hold the wound open. Using surgical instruments and lignocaine to numb the pain in deeper tissues, he controlled minor bleeding with locally-applied gelatine powder, using sterilised cotton thread to tie off larger vessels. After eight hours, however, he found that he could not get adequate exposure of his adrenals because moving his liver out of the way was unexpectedly painful. Exhausted, he bandaged the wound, cleaned up his room, and called the police to take him to hospital because of a 'rupture'.

When he arrived in the emergency room he handed the surgical registrar a detailed sheet of hand-written instructions of 'deep abdominal wound repair' and explained that he had been unable to complete the procedure. He was remarkably well in the circumstances and made a straightforward recovery. His psychiatrist, Dr Ned Kalin, said of him: 'The only hope is to engage him in intensive psychotherapy. At the same time, his urge to operate on himself must be brought under control. He does not see the relevance of such a difficult and laborious task and is much more comfortable spending hours in the medical library preparing for his next "curative" operation.'

June and Gerald　　　　　　　**by NAF**

YOU MUST BE JIM'S NEW GARDENER. I'M HIS NEIGHBOUR, GERALD.

HAD ANY LUCK WITH THE PETUNIAS THIS YEAR?

AREN'T THOSE JIM'S FEET STICKING OUT OF THE ORNAMENTAL POND?

CHILD
OF ANOTHER
TIME

*Bah! to Gary Glitter and Pooh! to platform heels and flares. For **ALICE PITMAN** the only true glamour was that of the era her mother recalled, of cats' whiskers, black-and-white flicks and bread and scratchit*

'The Aged P': Patricia Pitman with her daughter Alice and grandson Fred (above); Patricia Pitman in ATS uniform (left)

'Having a child when you're getting on is selfish,' I overheard someone say to a nodding companion on the 31 bus recently. I disagree. My mother had me in early middle-age, and having an oldie parent has definite advantages. Not for me parental reminiscences of getting stoned at hippy music festivals; nor of Elvis and the Cold War. What I got went even further back, into an evocative era of clipped accents, Jack Buchanan songs and *Children's Hour*.

Much as I appreciated the 1930s bread and dripping, wiggling-the-cat's-whisker type stories, it was the war stuff that really got my young blood going. I just couldn't get enough of it and prayed nightly for God to transport me from the daft teenybopper world of flares, Gary Glitter and Mud back to the age of London Underground stations during the Blitz, where I could belt out choruses of 'Run Rabbit Run' along with cheery cockneys drinking from chunky bottles of brown ale and smoking Woodbines.

My parents were both in the army during the war and lived through the V1 and V2 raids. The stories I was told, both funny and sad, never failed to grip me. My great-grandmother, for example, stomping back to the house in her bloomers, defiantly clenching her fist to the skies and declaring, 'I'm not going down no air-raid shelter, they can bomb me in me bed!' Or the day my parents narrowly escaped a V1 at Vauxhall, my father throwing himself and my mother to the compartment floor as shrouds of falling glass rained onto the platform – Dad furious to find my mother giggling helplessly because he looked so silly. As she recounted these wartime tales, I remember thinking it strange that my mother was flesh-coloured like me and not black and white like the films of that era.

I became utterly obsessed with the Second World War. Instead of queueing up for *Saturday Night Fever* like a normal child, I haunted the Imperial War Museum, where I'd gaze longingly at ATS uniforms, Vera Lynn song-sheets, ration books and Spitfires. I even recruited my younger cousin and dragged her along to my beloved 'Imp' whenever she came to stay. She was eventually just as obsessive as me.

Our walls were covered in posters of Winston Churchill, Battle of Britain pilots and old Hollywood film stars. My cousin was in love with Leslie Howard, while I swooned over James Stewart. Friends thought we were really weird; my mother, beaming with pleasure, would say how sensible we were. Into adolescence I continued to live and breathe the past. The songs I sang were those of Cole Porter or George Gershwin. I had the George Formby songbook on permanent loan from the library, teaching myself to play a toy ukulele and mimicking his extraordinary Lancashire accent. Watching David Lean's *Brief Encounter* was a sexy grown-up's paradise – much better than the heaving naked limbs you got in modern films – and I dreamt that I too would eventually find true love on a railway platform veiled in steam where my very own Trevor Howard, more daring than the film version, would chuck his wife ('small, delicate' Madeleine) for me. This film was responsible for my obsession with writing to old film stars. I penned a gushing letter to Celia Johnson, who wrote a kind note back in spindly old lady's handwriting. Two weeks later she died. (I read recently that she thought Trevor Howard was a bit stupid.)

James Mason was another victim. I wrote a feverish fan letter to him after seeing him thrashing Ann Todd's fingers with a whip as she tinkled the ivories in *The Seventh Veil*. He wrote back, enclosing a picture of a wrinkled old man. I remember being confused, before realising it was supposed to be him. Days after our brief correspondence, he too dropped off the hook. After that, my mother said that, for their sakes, it might be a good idea if I stopped writing to aged film stars.

> *Our walls were covered in posters of Winston Churchill, Battle of Britain pilots and old Hollywood film stars*

As an adult, having an oldie parent is a useful device for getting out of social engagements – 'Sorry, I'd love to come, but my mother's just fallen down the stairs.' The person I used this lie on sent my healthy, bemused parent a large bouquet of flowers with a Get Well Soon card.

As part of the dry martini generation, oldie parents still give you proper food, succulent meat and two veg, sneering at 'rabbit food' salads and other healthy alternatives. They never seem to get hangovers, they smoke like chimneys, they give you double gins even if you ask for lemonade, and just when you're wondering where you'd put the Alka Seltzer, they're opening another bottle of wine. They're also really good at film/telly trivia, plying you with useless but fascinating information. Did you know that that man tenderly kissing a woman in some vintage tear-jerker was arrested for gross indecency in a public lavatory in the early Fifties? 'He told the police he was a bank clerk, poor dear.' The other week, it was a John Garfield film: 'Ah, now he died in bed with a ballerina in 1949.'

It was my mother who told me that Margaret Rutherford got a kick out of having her husband serve her breakfast in bed wearing nothing but a miner's helmet; that Hitler's favourite film, which he'd watch over and over again, was *The Lives of a Bengal Lancer*; that when Laurel and Hardy sailed into Cork during a tour of Ireland, the bells of the town rang out their theme tune, moving them to tears. Oldie mothers should be applauded not sneered at. Giving birth in an old people's home is pushing it a bit, but late thirties/early forties seems a good time to have a child. The mother has lived a bit and doesn't resent her child for depriving her of youthful pleasures, and the child ends up with a mother who is wiser, worldlier and, like my mum, more interesting.

ISSUE 59, MAY 1994 BY STEVEN APPLEBY

ISSUE 33, MAY 1993 BY WILLIE RUSHTON

Hogarth's
Croatia

PAUL HOGARTH, *The Oldie's roving brushster, revisits the Middle Ages*

I had been a good oldie and donated a work to the Croatia Appeal of the International Monuments Trust. My picture, a watercolour of the castle-like Grand Hotel Dolder overlooking Lake Zurich, was snapped up by the hotel's owner for a handsome sum. Lawrence Durrell, who based the 'Paulhaus' – the psychiatric clinic in his novel *Nunquam* – on the Dolder, thought my picture might better make an illustration for a cautionary tale in *Struwwel-peter*. Be that as it may, I was delighted to receive an invitation from the Croatian Ministry of Tourism to depict the castles of the Zagorje. More of that later.

My first stop was Zagreb, heroic recipient of savage missile attacks earlier in 1995. On the face of it the city is bustling and prosperous. The baroque Upper Town resounds with yob-like shouts of graduating studentry; the Central Market and the cafés of the Lower Town are crowded with natives buying Spanish bananas and knocking back *strudla* with their espressos.

The Zagorje, 'the land beyond the mountains', lies some thirty miles northwest of Zagreb; a pleasant Ruritania dotted with numerous buildings from medieval times. After the Second World War, the local nobility fled and their castles and mansions were converted into hostels for delinquent teenagers or worse. Since independence, however, Croatia has developed a new pride in its heritage and seeks to make amends.

A few descendants of the old aristocracy bravely returned from Austria, Australia and the Americas to re-occupy their estates. Many, however, have not been reclaimed, and languish, stripped of oak panelling, ceramic stoves and forests. Others, like Bezaňec, the eighteenth-century seat of Baron Franjo Ksaver Ottenfels and his family, is now an excellent country hotel. A few, like Veliki Tabor, Trakošćan and Varaždin, still survive as national monuments.

Betwixt and between the fifty-odd ancient piles, a sturdy peasantry, invigorated by profitable sojourns as *Gastarbeiter* in Germany, cultivate modest plots of rich farmland, all well-maintained, with turkeys, geese and chickens running around. Each farmstead also has its own winehouse, where a peculiarly potent Riesling is on offer... Croatia has indeed rediscovered its heritage. But must every castle end up as a hotel? In the absence of a National Trust, they might. Entrepreneurs acquire dilapidated mansions at knockdown prices and await the tourist boom when war ends.

Below: drinks are served at Bosiljevo
Bottom left: trout fishing at Trakošćan

Busily doing NOTHING

Whatever happened to the lost art of the boulevardier, asks **ANTHONY SAMPSON,** *and where do you go if you want to become one?*

'**W**hat are you doing now?' I asked a distinguished architect, recently retired, expecting the usual protestations about 'never-been-busier-in-my-life' or 'can't-think-how-I-ever-had-time-for-a-job'. Instead he beamed and replied: 'I've become a boulevardier.'

I was overcome with curiosity and envy. The word conjured up a lost image of leisure, with much more romance than the English translation, 'man about town'. It conveyed a picture of Paris at the turn of the century, with dandies with silver-topped canes parading up and down the *grands boulevards* to attract the ladies, before they took a seat to join their friends in their café society.

How much more adventurous an occupation for a retiree than the British equivalent, the clubman! The club turns its ponderous back on the street, cultivates its exclusiveness with blackballs and rituals, and thrives on competitiveness and name-dropping. But the boulevard is the street, and the café is part of it, always waiting for newcomers and diversions.

> **The more spare time there is, the more it is dreaded and associated with failure and poverty**

How can boulevardism be revived? I asked some cosmopolitan friends. What training and qualifications are required?

Happening to be in Paris soon afterwards – travelling by the Eurostar to recapture the nineteenth-century spirit – I conducted some arduous field research. I spent time in the cafés looking out on the boulevards, investigating the current habitat, plumage and mating habits of the species.

There were no signs of silver-topped canes, bowing or kissing of hands. Even the pavements were not what they were. The once-fashionable northern boulevards – of the Italiens, St Denis and Haussmann – have been taken over (I was told) by immigrants who, having no jobs, are the real practitioners of leisure.

Most of the French, in fact, are even more obsessed than the British with appearing as busy as possible, with the help of every new kind of gadgetry – mobile telephones, calculators and laptop computers – which enable them to feel more American than the Americans.

In this futuristic world the nearest equivalent to the organised flirting of the old boulevards is the internet, which allows ambitious young Frenchmen to pick up promising young American women a few thousand miles away, and to start a provocative dialogue over their computer screens, reinforced by colour photographs to show off their charms.

But they are too busy comparing notes about their computer programmes to get down to more intimate

ILLUSTRATION BY WALLY FAWKES (AKA TROG)

discourse; and their competitiveness depends on speed, which allows little time for subtle seduction.

The true boulevardier flaunted his leisure. A century ago the rich displayed their wealth through their lack of work and their trappings and clothes which – as the great sociologist Thorstein Veblen analysed at the time – were the results of other people's work. But today the fear of unemployment has reversed all that. The more spare time there is, the more it is dreaded, and associated with failure and poverty: while over the last twenty years the rich have become obsessed with working and busy-ness – travelling, phoning, faxing, moving between offices – adopting all the activities of people who have to work to make a living. Even the luxury yacht, the old symbol of conspicuous consumption and total detachment, now has its communication centre, helicopter and satellite dish to keep constantly in touch with the mainland.

As the editor of the British magazine, the *Idler,* pointed out recently, the earlier periodicals all adopted names and styles which boasted of leisure – like the *Spectator,* the *Bystander* or the earlier *Idler* edited by Dr Johnson. But now most magazines are full of frenetic and competitive activity; and even the *Spectator* in its present incarnation is determined to be in the midst of the fray.

So what are the prospects for the would-be boulevardier? What happens to the oldie who has overworked for years to earn enough pension for luxurious leisure?

There is no doubt that he is entering the most difficult and exacting profession of all, which offers rewards like no other – a freedom from competitiveness, pressures and speed. But he will have to work at it.

Jeffrey Bernard
IS WELL

The old toper turns teetotaller

MAX GLATT, who runs the drug and alcohol addiction unit at St Bernard's hospital in Ealing, is recognised as one the world's leading authorities on alcoholism. He once wrote a book called *The Alcoholic and the Help He Needs*. What he should have done was write a book called 'The Abstainer and the Help He Needs'. My three-month spell in his ward was as unpleasant as anything I have ever experienced – with the possible exception of the company of drunks when I have been on the wagon – and I have been on it now for three months.

The penalty for this good behaviour is isolation, the absence of my friends and the lack of conversation with almost everyone I know since they appear to be drunk all the time. Can I have been so awful and boring myself? Yes. What is as bad is the fact that when I am not drinking I bore myself. I feel non-functional – a tea bag without hot water, bacon without an egg.

But it has never been my intention to get drunk. That has always been the inevitable accident at the end of the day. Most drugs either have side effects or they don't work efficiently. I used to start drinking at 11 am, pub opening time, and reach my peak of well being at lunch time. Unfortunately that peak only lasts for up to two hours and then the wheels fall off, the memory evaporates, repetitiveness sets in alongside aggression or melancholy or both. The only unpleasantness I now miss is the one of telling people home truths.

If I didn't find moderation to be so tedious I would say that it was the perfect state, but I must plump for being either poacher or gamekeeper. How did it all start with me, I often wonder, and when?

Hollywood and writers, nearly all of them American, certainly glamourised and even romanticised drinking, but we made the mistake of seeing Hemingway, for example, as a hero and not the ham that he in fact was. Mind you, I can't

think of anything more ghastly than the fact that were the Faulkners and O'Neills alive today they would be jogging from one health food shop to another. It would be like a celibate Erroll Flynn.

But Glatt's book is a bundle of laughs – unintentional ones – to me. In a chart mapping the downhill progress of the alcoholic he marks one station of the descent as 'Starts drinking with social inferiors'. People like Auberon Waugh do that every time they walk into a pub. But in spite of the fact that drunks may number among the most boring people in the world, one does meet some extraordinarily interesting people during the downhill struggle.

At the end of our three-month therapy in the hands of Max Glatt we all had to read our life stories, written during that time. Having read them out, other patients would raise questions and comment on them. I shall always remember that one idiot listened to mine and remarked, 'It seems to me, Jeff, that you are always reaching for the moon.' What else is there worth reaching for?

In the end Glatt never cured me. No one could. The only prerequisite to stopping drinking is to really want to. All I have managed to do since that experience is to control my alcoholism to a certain extent, and there is no virtue in my hitching a temporary ride on this wagon of mine. It has been forced on me by my pancreas which has become so enraged with me recently that it decided to haemorrhage.

It is a racing certainty that I shall drink again, probably some time quite soon. The likes of Glatt will put that down to what they call a 'personality defect'. They may be right but it is my way of blocking out this ghastly world. I had hoped that my current addiction to tea might have turned me into a workaholic, but no such luck. I am idle too. It is a tiresome business to be addicted to addiction. But I don't think I would change much – except for my pancreas.

Alighting on VENUS

Before the two books of diaries – The Prince, the Showgirl and Me (1995) and My Week With Marilyn (2000) – and before the 2011 Hollywood film, The Oldie published this extract from **COLIN CLARK**'s *diaries recalling his encounter with Marilyn Monroe...*

In 1956 Laurence Olivier and Marilyn Monroe were both incredibly famous. When it was announced that they were going to make a film together, it caused amazement and concern of a sort that is hard to imagine today. After all Miss Monroe was the epitome of the busty-but-brainless Hollywood blonde and Sir Laurence was the greatest classical actor of his generation etc, etc. It was really unthinkable that I should just walk into the offices of Laurence Olivier Productions, at the age of twenty-three, and demand a job. But that is what I did and, in the end, I got one.

My father, Kenneth Clark, was quite well known in intellectual circles then, and he and my mother were friends of 'Larry & Vivien'. Even so I must have been pretty brash – what my elder brother, Alan, still calls 'youthfully foolish' when I do something particularly stupid. It worked out well, though. The film was an incredible adventure despite the battles between the two so different cultures.

It was really a struggle between the old and the new. Despite his work in Hollywood, Olivier always thought of a film as a photographed play. And Marilyn, who had actually appeared in as many films as Olivier had at that time (25), was totally unaware of theatrical conventions, like learning lines in advance, and coming in on cue. The crew of the film, hand-picked by Olivier, thought of anything from America as vulgar and upstart (this was the Fifties, don't forget) and the idea of treating the movies as a brand-new medium was very threatening. I started by getting on very well with Marilyn and the whole American team. But I was always firmly in the Olivier camp, and just as well, for I was to remain as his personal assistant in the theatre for the next two years. I see now that it was Marilyn who was the 'film star', Marilyn, erratic as she was, who was the future.

Monday 16th July 1956

Problems – too much fakery: peroxide hair, dead white makeup, heavy lipstick, but that is her image. She looks confused too, lost, troubled. That's the MM [Marilyn Monroe] image too, I know, but even when she's shut the door on the reporters, she still looks in distress, not just acting it.

She doesn't seem to be able to shrug off the image in private, to throw off her coat, slump down on the sofa and say: 'Phew, let's have a drink.'

She gazes at AM [Arthur Miller] as if he is a superhero, but I don't think he is that nice. He's clearly very handsome and very attractive, but good-hearted, no. And she hasn't really got anyone else to depend on. A girl like that really needs her mum, but I'm told her mum is in a bin. Milton [Greene, executive producer] is clearly dependent on her, rushing round like all the others trying not to upset her, frightened of her even.

SLO [Sir Laurence Olivier] is much too remote. He's going to be her director and that should be a close relationship, but he is quite clearly not in any way concerned with her personally. He is the supreme professional, expecting and assuming that everyone else will be professional too...

I wish SLO could be cosy with MM. He's strong and romantic with most women but he only gets 'cosy' with men.

Wednesday 18th July

It goes without saying that she was late – but not very late, only half an hour... When MM did arrive we all got a shock – except Whitey [Allan Snyder, MM's personal makeup man], I suppose. She looked absolutely frightful. No makeup, just a skirt, a tight blouse, head scarf and dark glasses. Nasty complexion, a lot of facial hair, shape-less figure and, when the glasses came off, a very vague look in her eye. No wonder she is so insecure.

She bolted into her dressing-room with Milton and Whitey and stayed there for twenty minutes. Eventually they coaxed her out, looking very tense indeed, and walked her to the small studio. The whole idea is to film her first without makeup on, so she sat on a stool, under the bright lights, like a prisoner of war...

Thursday 19th July

MM late again but this time no one cared. Everyone was only thinking about the 'rushes' – the film that was shot yesterday. At 9.30 Milton and SLO led the way into the viewing theatre, and we all held our breath. Jack [Cardiff, lighting cameraman] and Whitey had already seen it together, early on. They were looking pretty smug but said nothing...

The film was magical, and there's no other way to describe it. The stuff we shot in the morning, although it resembled a police line-up mug shot, was quite heartbreaking. MM looked like a young delinquent girl, helpless and vulnerable under the harsh lights. The afternoon footage was even more extraordinary. What an incredible transformation. Now MM looked like an angel – smooth, glowing, eyes shining with joy (Jack's lights), perfect lips slightly parted, irresistible. Quite a few people had wandered in to look and they were stunned. We all fell in love there and then.

Tuesday 14th August

Dame S [Sybil Thorndike] had a long line about Eleanor Duse being a much greater actress than Sarah Bernhardt. MM simply could not remember when to reply. Dame S is babbling on and ends with a rhetorical question: 'You agree. No?'

All MM had to say was 'No' at the right moment, but today even this proved too complicated... Halfway through, SLO tried a controlled explosion. MM was stunned, as usual, but SLO had reckoned without Dame S who promptly gave him a good ticking off. 'Don't you realise what a strain this poor girl is under? She hasn't had your years of experience. She is far from home in a strange country, trying to act in a strange part. Are you helping or bullying?' Poor SLO, who naturally thinks he is the injured party, was stunned.

MM was radiant. 'Oh thank you so much, Dame Sybil. But I mustn't forget my lines. I promise I'll try to remember them from now on.' And she was good as gold for the rest of the afternoon.

Wednesday 15th August

I suppose you could say that today was a red-letter day. This morning I definitely saw more of MM than I ever expected to, and she went up in my estimation in more ways than one. She arrived really early, for her, and nearly caught us on the hop at 7.30 am. She was still in a jolly mood – I expect she and AM had had a good laugh over SLO's discomfiture.

As lunchtime drew near David [Orton, assistant director] caught me in the corridor, and told me to look for MM's marked script which was missing. I assumed this meant MM was on the set so I just barged into her dressing-room and straight into the inner sanctum. What David had not told me was that filming had already ended.

There stood MM, completely nude, with only a white towel round her head.

I stopped dead. All I could see were beautiful white and pink curves. I must have gone as red as a beetroot. I couldn't even turn and rush out, so I just stood there and stared and stammered.

MM gave me her most innocent smile. 'Oh Colin,' she said. 'And you an Old Etonian!'

How did she stay so cool? And how did she know which school I had gone to and what it meant? When I managed to get out of the room and pull myself together, I realised that behind the fog MM could be a bit brighter than we all think.

Monday 19th November

When MM left the studio, she did so quickly and furtively. She is supposed to come back tomorrow but we all know she won't. She didn't say goodbye to anyone, not even her personal dresser, who has been so loyal and patient, or to Gordon, her hairdresser.

We knew we would never see her again and, sad to tell, it was an immense relief.

Poor Milton is very depressed. He feels a failure, but he would have needed the strength of ten men to have succeeded in all his roles. He had been warned about what he was taking on by other producers of MM's films. But her appeal is so great that he shrugged them off.

Even MM is not to blame. The great engine of publicity that surrounds her is unstoppable. Like some awful curse of the gods, it stalks her every moment, and one day it will crush her.

'98, 99, 100… Coming, ready or not!'

Cartoon by: Rosko

AUBERON WAUGH

RAGE

Thirty-two years ago, when the Waugh family started taking its summer holidays in the part of agricultural southern France they call the Pays d'Oc, every village in the neighbourhood had its village idiot. In those days, French villages were quite backward by English standards, and all the village washing was done by hand in a communal cold-water tub fed from a spring. It never occurred to anyone to lock the village idiot away in a special home for the educationally challenged, with idealistic, specially trained young women to talk to them slowly in patronising welfare accents. They just loped around the village, sometimes making a nuisance of themselves and breaking things, sometimes engaging people in conversation of a sort, but always accepted as what is nowadays called part of the community.

A similar fate awaited those who lived too long and became senile. On sunny days they were pushed out of doors, and anybody passing would greet them, receiving a grunt back, or the rolling of an eye, or more probably no acknowledgement at all. In the winter they were kept indoors in the kitchen, wrapped in filthy sacking, and left to dribble quietly in a corner until someone – the daughter-in-law, more often than not – went to spoon in some soup.

It was not tremendously dignified, perhaps, by our modern ideas, but it was a great deal less gloomy than the rows of recumbent forms on drips, lying in a coma, recognising no one, turned once in the morning and once in the evening like newly cut hay. These forms represent our furthest advance in the science of caring for the aged. The point about senility is that it is only distressing if people are prepared to be distressed by it. In the small villages of the Aude, in southern France, they simply weren't prepared

to treat it as anything except a fact of life, to be regretted, sworn at or joked about as the spirit moved them. In England, it seems to me that we treat senility as something between a disgrace and an infectious disease, possibly brought on by masturbation in youth. Not only are oldies who begin to show the symptoms whisked away into a home, even if it means ruining the family in the process; once they are in a home, they become a non-person, visited grudgingly and with increasing embarrassment on both sides.

> **The point about senility is that it is only distressing if people are prepared to be distressed by it**

This is not just a reflection on our peculiar family relationships. It is institutionalised in the fabric of the nation. When distinguished oldies become senile, they are immediately withdrawn from view, not left babbling in the sun. Harold Wilson was scarcely seen in his last five years, while he was suffering from Alzheimer's. It seems especially craven to lock a former Prime Minister away in this fashion when we have a national institution called the House of Lords, specially designed for them to exhibit themselves. This is one of the most humane political initiatives in the world.

When I visited the Upper House on business two weeks ago, I was surprised to see a very elderly peer pushed past me in an invalid chair with his jaw tied shut by a bandage over his head. I could not make out whether it had been put there because he had died or in order to gag him. In either event, it was much more humane to wheel

him around than to shut him away in a funny farm or a mortuary.

Which brings us back to Harold Wilson. A new theory going the rounds to explain his mysterious resignation in 1976 has it that he felt the first intimations of Alzheimer's disease at the beginning of the year, remembered that his mother had suffered from it at the same age – sixty – and decided to resign on the spot rather than disgrace himself. He is thought to have given this explanation to Dr Thomas Stuttaford, a former MP who is now medical columnist for *The Oldie* and the *Times*.

This seems to me most unlikely. I don't believe he had the faintest intimation of Alzheimer's any more than any of us do when we find we have temporarily forgotten our spouse's name. He had the best part of another twenty years to live. Far more likely that he was threatened with exposure as a security risk unless he resigned by the then Director of MI5. That is what I have always maintained.

The simple reason for all these problems of old age is that most of us are living far too long. There is one nostrum which keeps Alzheimer's at bay which also, on average, shortens life by a few years. That is cigarette smoking. If Wilson had not felt bound to establish his proletarian credentials by smoking a pipe (like poor mad Tony Benn, but nobody will ever notice whether he has Alzheimer's or not) but smoked cigarettes instead, he might not have lived any longer but he would not have died so shamefacedly nor so secretively.

Everybody should be encouraged to start smoking cigarettes on their sixtieth birthday. If I become Minister of Health, I shall make cigarettes available on prescription from that date, along with cannabis. Wilson's last years could have been made happier if he had received the right medical advice in 1976.

Old Tilly's Teapot

A rustic tale of heavenly beauty and impious thoughts by **WINIFRED FOLEY**

It stood in its little glass-fronted cupboard, well out of reach of meddlesome hands, on the wall of the downstairs room of old Tilly's one-up one-down cottage. It was undoubtedly the loveliest inanimate object in the impoverished little mining village, coveted and admired by every female eye from young child upwards. It was a delicate china teapot ornately decorated with roses, including one for the knob of the lid. The handle was formed of twining leaves and the base edged with a ring of rosebuds – all exquisitely coloured and emphasised with gold paint. It had been given to Tilly in an impulsive gesture of generosity by one of her wealthy employers, who considered it too ornately vulgar for her own aesthetic tastes.

Its ownership had given the lowly placed Tilly a status of some consequence in her own eyes. Tilly was already a seventy-year-old arthritic when she came to the village with her teapot and bits and pieces to rent the tiny cottage for two shillings a week. Orphaned at ten years old, she had been sent into domestic service. During sixty working years she had accrued some frugal savings, a fiercely independent spirit and a capacity for work far beyond her physical frailty. She tilled every inch of her small garden, gathered all her fuel from the surrounding forest and augmented her savings by earning a shilling a week for cleaning the village chapel until, in her eighties, her twisted limbs could no longer cope. Then Lloyd George brought into law the munificent blessing of a five shillings a week pension for the over-seventies and ensured Tilly's independence.

During those twenty years Tilly had withstood all the cajoling, flattery, and all sorts of offers from such people as the chapel minister's wife, to hang onto her precious teapot. All but the most determined and hardened coveters had given up hope and retired from the fray. The two left had become obsessional about getting the ownership. Tilly had made no promises to anyone, but Mrs Herbert from the next-door cottage felt she had a moral and righteous claim when the old lady eventually died. True, Tilly always tried to pay something for the little services her now bedridden state made necessary – but Fanny Herbert felt she went far beyond the boundary of ordinary neighbourliness. Didn't she empty the old woman's slop bucket in the privy hole in her own garden, fetch her water from the village well, frequently take lumps of coal from her own shed to put on Tilly's fire, and take in titbits of food for her?

As for that Minnie Hatton who did bugger all for the old girl, except when she heard the old thing was sinking – then up she came all smarm and charm with a saucerful of custard – calling the old girl Aunt Tilly, and her nothing but the niece of old Tilly's cousin Alf who had emigrated to Australia as a young man... 'Blood is thicker than water' – and she had a legal right to that teapot, she had been reported as saying.

Quite a few saucers of Minnie's custard had come Tilly's way when her frail misshapen skin-and-bone old body appeared to be giving up. And village gossip being what it is, as news of her illness went round the village, it had

ILLUSTRATION BY CRAMER

killed her off a few times before it got back to her cottage and found her still alive. But this time it seemed old Tilly's spirit was surrendering to the inevitable. She had been sleeping downstairs for the last couple of years and now lay apparently in a coma – she showed no interest in Minnie's custard or Fanny's not-to-be-outdone bit of rice pudding. The sun streamed in from a hot cloudless July sky. The door and window were wide open. The two women sat quiet in their mutual hate and rivalry, both acutely aware of the laboured breathing coming from the bed. 'My poor Aunt – it looks as though 'er be goin' this time. Thank God I shall 'ave summat to remember 'er by, for 'er promised me that teapot was mine when 'er'd gone.'

'That be a brazen lie. 'Er can't abide the sight o' thee; 'er told me so – you was the last person 'er'd give it to. "You be the only friend I've got," 'er told me many a time, and 'er allus looked up at that teapot when 'er said it. I know 'er meant that I should 'ave it.'

As the faces of the two protagonists flushed up purple with rage, the pallor of death descended on old Tilly and the death rattle came with her last breath. Exactly at that moment the glass door in front of the teapot shattered, and with it the precious content behind. Now it was the two women who went ghastly pale (both were chapel-goers) – this was the hand of God punishing them for breaking the commandment 'Thou shalt not covet...'

Alfie Phillips was scuffling among the stones in the rough pathway surrounding the village, looking for a suitable sized one for his grand new catapult, brought home for him by his big brother in the army. With the careless callousness of boyhood he scanned the branches of the trees edging the path for a sitting bird target. He was quite sure he had only missed by a fraction that big blackbird perched on the lilac tree in front of old Tilly's cottage... Though absorbed in his search, he looked up at the approaching figure. It was Minnie Hatton – but what the devil was the matter with her? Her teeth were chattering as though it was a bitterly cold day, her eyes were wide with terror, and she was as white as though she had seen a ghost. Serve her right if she had. Nobody liked Minnie Hatton. His Mam reckoned she was nothing but a gossip-mongering hypocrite.

My First Job

by journalist and broadcaster SANDY GALL

BEFORE JOINING ITN in 1963, I worked for Reuters for ten years in Germany, the Middle East and Africa. So I knew I was a pretty good foreign correspondent. But every time I contemplated standing in front of a camera and spouting a few trenchant words, I had a nasty bout of butterflies in the stomach.

On my second or third day in the office, I was asked to cut my teeth on the Post Office Exhibition, which in that particular year was celebrating the opening of the new, round-the-world submarine cable. It was the sort of boring, eminently droppable story they gave you on your first assignment.

My cameraman was an ex-newsreel stalwart called Jackie Howard, who made up in irascibility what he lacked in inches; his soundman, Frank McNally, was equally opinionated, I soon discovered, and they started arguing as soon as we drove off in the camera car.

But once he had put poor old Frank firmly in his place – as cameramen like to do with soundmen – Jackie exuded bonhomie, inducting me into the arcane mysteries of filming, and good-naturedly demonstrating GVs (general views), close-ups and cutaways. All went effortlessly, only the interview remaining. The man in charge of the exhibition was standing by nervously, running his finger round the inside of his collar.

'Where are we going to do the interview, Jackie?' I asked, feeling the butterflies taking wing in my stomach. 'Somewhere quiet,' I added beseechingly.

About two hundred people were filing round the big room, peering at the various exhibits. Jackie drew himself up to his full height of five feet, five inches and bellowed: 'Quiet please, everybody. We're going to record an interview.'

A hush fell on the room and everyone turned to stare. I found myself fervently wishing the old cliché would come true: that the ground really would open at my feet and swallow me up.

'Ready when you are, Mr DeMille,' Jackie boomed, enjoying being the centre of attention.

> *In front of the camera, I had a nasty bout of butterflies in the stomach*

My hand shook so much that I could hardly hold the microphone, a large, awkwardly-shaped, bulbous monstrosity. I stammered some inane question. The interviewee started to gabble furiously. I found myself unable to concentrate on what he was saying, aware that two hundred people were listening to every word.

Eventually I heard myself saying 'Thank you very much, Mr So-and-so...' He stared at me disbelievingly. 'I believe you were every bit as nervous as I was,' he said loudly. I pretended to laugh off such a silly remark. But, to my shame, I knew he was right. At that moment, I hated myself, and I hated television even more.

NIB ERRANT

MICHAEL CUMMINGS *is the only cartoonist to have caricatured every Prime Minister since the end of the Second World War*

You may well wonder what masochistic impulse has made me chronicle the actions of a collection of people, most of whom have conducted this country to its present sorry state. The answer is, I wanted to be a cartoonist from childhood, and my political journalist father, A J Cummings of the *News Chronicle*, fired my enthusiasm.

Michael Foot was my first editor, for whom I drew cartoons for *Tribune*. After six of these cartoons were published, I was approached by a member of his staff who said his colleagues were very worried because the cartoons attacking Stalin and the Soviets were so right-wing. He couldn't understand 'what had got into Michael Foot' in publishing them. Not exactly the Michael Foot of the ludicrous allegations of him being a KGB agent!

After this episode I wrote to Lord Beaverbrook asking for a job. He sent

me back a cordial note saying he was 'just an old man who now had nothing to do with the papers and spent his days in the sun'. But he gave me an appointment to see the editor of the *Daily Express*, Arthur Christiansen. He took me on, and thereafter I stayed on the *Express* for 41 years and a succession of twelve stimulating editors. I was also taken on by the redoubtable John Junor of the *Sunday Express*. Like everybody in the newspaper business, I had many ups and downs. One particular 'down' was when the unions stopped the *Scottish Daily Express* from publication because they didn't like the political content of a cartoon.

Lord Beaverbrook occasionally didn't like the content of my cartoons, but he never stopped one being published. Though once he asked me to stop caricaturing de Gaulle for a while. I'd recently done a particularly critical drawing about the General which so incensed the French government that

they lodged an official protest from the Quai d'Orsay. They were suspicious that Harold Macmillan was masterminding an anti-French campaign in revenge for de Gaulle's 'No!' to Britain joining the Common Market.

Clockwise from main image: Cummings with ten Prime Ministers; Sister Wendy Beckett.; Melvyn Bragg; John Buchan

Winston Churchill, however, was a politician who did like my political message when I poked fun at Attlee's socialist government. I'd invented a spoof Hampstead-style Labour MP (called 'Zilliboy Shinbag') who every day made a fool of the socialists by making foot-in-the-mouth statements – a sort of left-wing John Gummer. Beaverbrook told me I was Churchill's favourite cartoonist, and he invited me to dinner to meet the great man. Churchill gave me a searching interrogation on how I did my job. As he was so keen on painting, I wondered if he'd be tempted to try his hand at caricature.

A politician who was sensitive to being caricatured was the Leader of the Labour Party, Hugh Gaitskell. At a party conference he once approached me with a charming smile and outstretched hand, saying I was the only person in a group of journalists he did not know. When I told him my name, his smile was extinguished, he withdrew his hand, turned his back and abruptly marched upstairs to his hotel bedroom.

By contrast, socialist politician Emanuel Shinwell told me, 'My boy, however much you irritate a politician by lampooning him in a cartoon, he'll be much more irritated if you leave him out of your cartoons!'

Mrs Thatcher probably approved of me because she asked me for a couple of originals. One of them was a scathing attack on the Foreign Office. This says something about her opinion of the Foreign Office.

Another super-controversial politician was Enoch Powell. When he made his 'rivers of blood' speech attacking immigration, I drew a cartoon suggesting that what he said was what most people were thinking. I drew him being accused in the High Court of the crime of 'telling the truth'. I received over 200 letters from readers congratulating me on the cartoon.

However, some months later, Powell made a speech suggesting repatriation for immigrants. For this, I did a cartoon showing Macmillan being repatriated to his native Scotland and the Royal Family being repatriated to its origins in Germany. This cartoon provoked over 100 letters from angry readers because I dared to mock the words of St Enoch.

In the course of their careers cartoonists often invent a character. Many years ago an election campaign started up, and Arthur Christiansen told me that everybody was worried about rising prices, so I must invent a figure symbolising them. I conjured up an immensely tall, thin, sinister figure called 'Mr Rising Price'. This was reproduced from the bottom to the topmost part of the big *Daily Express* broadsheet page. It was carried on every day in ever-expanding guises, and was instantly a terrific success, capturing the mood of the readers. It continued to appear for many years and is still referred to.

The irony is that when I invented Mr Rising Price, inflation was minute compared with the hyper-inflation launched by Macmillan, Heath, Lawson and the rest.

People often say to me that today is a good time for my profession because there's so much to cartoon about. Unfortunately, the world is so lunatic that it's going way beyond exaggeration and satire. So many British institutions, groups, politicians and individuals have abandoned common sense to embrace the idiocies of political correctness, trendy technology and other follies. They are like the lunatic asylum inmates who won't sit down because they believe they have glass bottoms.

Even the great satirist Malcolm Muggeridge, were he still alive, might conceivably have been reduced to silence contemplating such an embarrassment of riches of idiocy. In such an environment cartoonists can also feel slightly redundant.

Michael Cummings
1919–1997

Michael Cummings died in October 1997 aged 78. A veteran from the *Daily Express* and the Muggeridge *Punch*, he was a regular illustrator of *The Oldie's* TV column and books pages from the very beginning until shortly before his death.

God...

by Alice Thomas Ellis

I recently asked a young – well, youngish – friend (42 to be exact) what she thought of feminists. 'Hate them,' she responded tersely. She is an editor on a New York magazine, elegant, witty, confident and acknowledging no debt to the Sisters. She reminds me very much of certain film stars of the Thirties and Forties – Katharine Hepburn, Joan Crawford, Bette Davis, etc, none of whom resemble in the least the downtrodden wimps so crucial to feminist myth. Modern Woman was coming along nicely until after the war, when Baby Doll emerged – Lord knows where from – to be counterbalanced by the Amazon who, even if she did not slice off a breast, burned her bra (which, when you come to consider it, was foolish, since if you are going in for drawing bows a little structural support in the background can only be beneficial). Disgruntled females organised 'consciousness raising sessions' and adopted other outmoded and discredited Marxist tactics, so that in a while everyone hated them, though few dared to admit it. A dreadful breed of feminist men arose, claiming to sympathise with this struggle for justice, and everyone hated them too.

Social engineering is not a good idea. Human nature just will not have it. In LA a few years ago I sat with a group of ladies round a lunch table. They wore the baffled and aggrieved expression of hyenas who cannot understand why their prey is proving elusive. They all had jobs but no men and they could not imagine why this should be so. They had done all the right things – loved and esteemed themselves highly, explained to men what chauvinist pigs they

were, been to assertiveness classes and thought hard before shaving their legs. Those with an ex-husband demanded that he support them for the rest of their lives, no matter what the relative state of their salaries, and then wondered despairingly why most men appeared to be homosexual. They were unaware of the extent of their unattractiveness: their greed, their humourlessness, their whingeing, their lack of generosity and the unsightly cut of their jackets.

Many of them still give the impression of being clinically insane. A group recently carted round a church crucifix with a female on it – happily not a real one – referring to the curious thing as Jesa Crista. Sheer, pure nuttiness can go no further. Never mind that it's blasphemous, it is silly to suggest that historical figures can change sex. Was General Custer a girl? Mussolini a madam? The recorded circumcision of Our Lord was used as evidence against the early heresies as proof of his humanity. It must surely also serve as evidence of his maleness.

I have another question I should like answered. What if God had chosen to send a daughter to redeem us? What would the feminists say to that? You can bet your boots – and your hat and coat and gloves – that they'd be whining that women had to do everything; men were just absolutely hopeless and never did anything useful. Here was this poor woman suffering unspeakable agonies for us and what were the men doing, eh? One 'feminist theologian' (*sic*) I spoke to gave it as her opinion that if Our Lord couldn't be represented as female then females couldn't be sure that they were redeemed. I know people are thick but surely they can't be as thick as that. As long as equality is construed as meaning 'identical' we are going down skidding on good intentions to the inky bottom. The Cardinal, a well-meaning soul, has just said something about the Church 'going forward' – an unfortunate concept to apply to an edifice built upon a rock. If it starts paddling like a poodle in all directions after whatever fad or fancy is presently beguiling the 'intellectuals', it will collapse into nothing more than a pizza parlour (a nightmare predicted in the light of newly built churches) and everyone can choke on their chosen flavour.

It's summer, so the Meanie's garden is full of roses and the roses are full of greenfly. Before unleashing chemical warfare, try spraying the plants with water in which you have boiled lemon, lime and orange rind. Aphids absolutely hate citrus oil. Steeping several cloves of garlic in water with a tablespoon of chilli flakes is another frugal and organic replacement for toxic bug blasters.

JANE THYNNE

ILLUSTRATION BY MARTIN HONEYSETT

Unwrecked England
The Downs

Candida Lycett Green

On a pale watery day, depressed, I walked from Uffington towards the high wall of Downs a mile to the south. The footpath led across flat fields to meet the clear chalk-bottomed stream which falls from a spring below Uffington Wood. Elder and hawthorn arched beside the path and an occasional huge crab-apple tree towered over it, spread under with a thick carpet of rotting fruit. The Old Berks Hunt had been this way the day before: hounds' feet had patterned the mud and flattened dead nettle stalks; horses' hooves had churned a deep furrow along the side of a field of kale. At the stile they had turned away towards the hamlet of Fawley and I followed the path instead, which led up through sheep pasture and across an old stone bridge beside a ford.

As the path climbed the steep incline beyond, the stream fell into a deeper and deeper cutting, tumbling down in a series of waterfalls until it was lost from sight in a mossy elder-filled ravine and the path petered out in an open field. From here, there was a perfect level view of the strange and ethereal hill where St George is said to have killed the dragon – like a flat-topped steamed pudding moulded onto the lower slopes of the Downs. The chalk marks down its sides are the dragon's blood.

Across the Icknield Way, which at this stretch between Kingston Lisle and Ashbury carves its way under the hill, lurching in and out of fairground-like dips and bends, is a proper humdinger of a farm called Britchcombe. The small brick and clunch house clings to the eastern side of the combe, and behind it an ash wood, veiled in old man's beard, hangs all around and goes up a steep hollow to the sky. The sloping yard harbours higgledy-piggledy barns, battered and unglamorous, and a pretty eighteenth-century chequered brick dovecote. Under apple trees are game hens, peacocks, ducks, geese, chickens, guinea fowl and, in hutches and sheds, rare breeds of sheep like Castlemilk Morrits and North Ronaldsays.

At this time of year more often than not you will find the farmer bottlefeeding the newborn lambs in one of the barns. She has lived on the farm since the early Thirties and can recite local poetry, from 'The Barkshire Tragedy' to 'The Lay of the Hunted Pig', until the cows come home. She runs nearly a thousand sheep on the Downs around her farm which includes White Horse Hill.

The only way out of Britchcombe to the top of the Downs is by climbing the steep bank, clinging to a rope of old ivy as thick as a bannister rail, where a stile marks the way out into an open field which runs up the side of the wood. Halfway up this last slope there is a plateau to rest, where an old deep-cut chalk track runs curling up from Fawler Combes to join the path. You can look back at the village of Kingston Lisle settled comfortably below, with its four-square farm and its elegant eighteenth-century pile just visible through the trees of the park.

The last pull is easy and the generous track between the plough, where peewits call, leads to the irresistible, timeless, archaic Ridgeway – the oldest track in Europe. All is right with the world up here. The feeling that men have travelled this way for perhaps ten thousand years or more puts things in perspective, and it doesn't matter that the cold wind whistles over from Lambourn.

I walked down by White Horse Hill, where Thomas Hughes, Uffington's famous nineteenth-century son, loved to be and of which he wrote in *Tom Brown's Schooldays*:

'And then what a hill is White Horse Hill! There it stands right up above all the rest, 900 feet above the sea, and the boldest, bravest shape for a chalk hill that you ever saw... The ground falls rapidly on all sides. Was there ever such turf in the whole world?... It is a place you won't ever forget – a place to open a man's soul and make him prophesy...'

ILLUSTRATION BY JOHN O'CONNOR

I was a Crazy Gang Chorus Girl ★

Way back when there was no alternative to comedy, **MARIE LINDSAY-HOGG** *trod the boards of the Victoria Palace with Nervo and Knox, Naughton and Gold, and Bud Flanagan*

I can smell the greasepaint now. Leichner 5 & 9 and I've forgotten what else, but that smell...! I was having lunch with my old friend Gai Pearl and we were reminiscing. We'd been together in *Knights of Madness*, the Crazy Gang show at the Victoria Palace in the early Fifties.

'Do you remember when Charlie Naughton locked me in the loo?' said Gai. 'No. What happened?' 'I missed two numbers. I was on Punishment Call and fined! At least he paid my fine though.'

Gai and I hadn't met for years; we'd lost touch and found each other again by sheer chance. She had gone on to become a famous dancer in Italy, married, and was now big in PR for Italian fashion houses. I'd had a husband and lots of children in Norfolk.

'Then, another time,' she continued, 'in "Dig-a-Doo", the whole row of us danced onto the stage in Zulu costume with black curly wigs – I was in the middle – and suddenly I was yanked to a standstill. My wig hooked up on the scenery and I went through all the motions on the spot for the rest of the number. The solo up front wondered what on earth the audience was laughing at.'

The Crazy Gang Shows had been revived after the war by Jack Hylton, and *Knights of Madness* ran for two and a half years. The Gang at that time consisted of Nervo and Knox, Naughton and Gold, and Bud Flanagan – in his battered straw hat and enormous old racoon coat. Chesney Allen, Bud's partner, had retired, ill, in 1946. Freddie Bretherton conducted the orchestra and Grace Draper, Gillian Roma and Linda Lee were the leading ladies. Sundry speciality acts filled the gaps. I was one of six showgirls picked for good voices, height and looks. Together with a dozen or so dancers, girls and boys, we provided the glamour in the brilliant twice-nightly explosion of lights and colour and music and fun.

One night in the second performance, the six of us strutted onto the stage singing 'Musical Demon', a Twenties number. We wore tight black satin dresses fringed with white, white satin cloche caps and high-heeled, cross-laced white shoes. Except me. My plain black courts stood out like a sore thumb. Or two. Oh Lord! I almost lost my smile, for the consequences would be dire.

After the number, back in the dressing room, the Tannoy crackled into life. 'Miss Foster... Prompt Corner In The Interval PLEASE!' It was the stage manager speaking in C-A-P-I-T-A-L letters and he wasn't known as 'Adolf Hitler' for nothing. I was sentenced to be at the theatre at half-past nine the next morning on Punishment Call. Nine thirty! By the time I got back to my digs, had dinner and time to unwind it was nearly four o'clock in the morning! I needed my lie-in and having to get up at seven o'clock was punishment in itself.

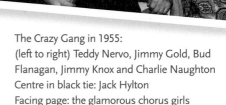

The Crazy Gang in 1955:
(left to right) Teddy Nervo, Jimmy Gold, Bud Flanagan, Jimmy Knox and Charlie Naughton
Centre in black tie: Jack Hylton
Facing page: the glamorous chorus girls

Despite bus and train delays I was there on time. So was Adolf (he'd had to get up early too), and what a telling off I got! I then had to sit in the semi-dark stalls until released, thoroughly diminished, an hour or so later. I was too naïve and vulnerable in those days to protest. You could be forgiven for thinking that this all happened in borstal during the inmates' annual concert.

> **Most of us, most of the time, didn't have boy-friends. We thought it odd: we were all so dishy!**

The girls' dressing rooms were on the far side of the stage up a narrow winding stone staircase. We showgirls had the middle room. Mirrors stuck with telegrams and good luck cards and bordered with bright lights ranged down one wall; the long dressing table held makeup boxes, pots of cream and powder, mascots, and all the paraphernalia marking our individual places. On the opposite wall and on a rail at the far end near the washbasins hung our voluminous costumes, cared for by Barbara, our beloved dresser-cum-'Mum'. Between frantic changes she sat and knitted, listened to our woes and chatter and made our interval tea.

Most of us, most of the time, didn't have boyfriends. The audiences wouldn't have believed this and we, too, thought it odd; we were all so dishy! Most of us were virginally innocent – reluctantly, to judge by our conversation, which veered from this phenomenon to the love life of whoever was lucky enough to have one. Great excitement erupted when one of us arrived starry-eyed about a marvellous man she'd met. We'd all rush out after the show to give him the once over as he waited for her at the stage door.

Tall, elegant Frances told us one Monday that she had met Ray Milland at a party that weekend. She was surprisingly cagey and blushed a lot, confessing that he'd paid her a great deal of attention and called her a beautiful English rose. She had agreed to go out with him after the show. We were sworn to secrecy and all promised faithfully not to stare if we saw him waiting. He really was there, leaning on a lamp post on the opposite side of the road, looking for all the world like Ray Milland in a Hollywood movie, coat collar turned up and the brim of his trilby pulled down, hands deep in his pockets.

The next evening in the dressing room, we clamoured for details but didn't get them. Frances blushed even more and quietly said she'd had a lovely time. It was different in those days. Romance was the thing. Sex was still pretty private and 'the media' hadn't been invented. We read in the paper later that Mr Milland had returned to the States – and to his wife.

Fay was a different kettle of fish altogether. She was large, loud, exceptionally pretty and very white-skinned. Her steady boyfriend came and went as his job directed. One weekend they'd made the most of his return and she arrived late for the Monday evening show, wide-eyed and worried. The rest of us were made-up and waiting in bras and pants ready to don our first costumes. Fay stripped off. We gasped and hooted. 'Oh help!' she moaned.

'Do you mind if I exist?'

She was covered in love bites. Brilliant black and purple ones all over her shoulders, neck, arms and thighs.

'Fifteen minutes, please,' called a voice over the Tannoy, and we all sprang into action.

'You do your face!' I yelled at Fay. 'Come on, Fran, you do that side and I'll do this.' For ten frantic minutes I daubed makeup on the love bites on one side and Fran did the same on the other, while Fay, with difficulty, struggled in the middle to do her face. She looked only slightly less piebald when we'd finished and had to brave the witticisms of the Gang and others until the marks faded a long time later.

I reminded Gai about the café opposite the Victoria Palace stage door. We used to congregate there before the show, dancers and showgirls and others from about 4.30 pm onwards. Friendships were started here – and finished. Assignations were made, gossip exchanged and grievances aired. There was invariably a weedy man at another table ogling the girls (or the boys) but nobody minded. Those days we felt safe. No matter how late I left the theatre – and it was never before 11.30 pm – I had no qualms about travelling back to my digs alone, walking quite some way in the dark from the station.

Gai reminded me about a Sunday shortly before the show folded. She'd telephoned to ask me to go with her that night to a party on board a P&O ship in East Ham Docks. I was to be the blind date of the host, the young Second Officer. I went...

Reader, I married him.

Modern life

What is... marketing?

MODERN LIVES are being remorselessly crushed beneath the blind executive rump; its twin white buttocks are management and accountancy, between which escapes the thin mephitic steam of marketing.

Marketing men are the bogus priests and snake-oil men of modern commerce. Their trade is a shitty combination of wishful thinking, statistical jiggery-pokery and the jitters, which elements they manipulate with the glib plausibility of a street-corner three-card-trickster, though instead of finding the lady, they find the lowest common denominator.

If you asked a marketing man what he actually did, his instincts would direct him to question 1,732 randomly selected individuals in the target population as to what they thought he did, and present that to you in the form of a laser-printed, perfect-bound Report complete with pie-charts, graphics and outline numbering without which no marketing man can face the world. (I'm Michael; how d'you do?' 'Ah, I'm glad you asked that. 2. I'm Chip. 2(a) I'm in marketing, 2(a)(i) for my sins; 2(b) what's your line exactly? (3) Great. Super. Cheers.')

We used to see a government or great enterprise as a ship. Now, command has been seized by deracinated 'executives' who, having spent their working lives climbing the greasy pole, possess no other skills than greasy-pole climbing, and are hiding in the Captain's cabin, swigging up the drink and negotiating to flog off the engines. The accountants – unsocialised, mole-like men who once toiled honourably in the bowels making sure the steam pressure didn't drop and there was always enough coal – have been invited on to the bridge; now they scamper from portside to starboard, tapping the dials and writing down the readings; but they do not know which one is the compass, and there's no point looking outside because all the charts have been sold. Some primitive faculty of imitation has shown these miserable 'men' that, although navigation need not actually be done, it should at least appear to be done. This task has been given to marketing men, who perform it by carrying out surveys of the passengers, asking them where they would like to go, and where they think they might be at the moment.

The passengers' answers – unblemished by any hint of actual knowledge – are subjected to expert statistical analysis, then got up in the form of a laser-printed report (illustrated with computer graphics, pie charts, bell-curves, logos and inspirational pictograms), which is then pushed under the door of the Captain's cabin. And when the ship hits the rocks, there can be no blame, because everything that could be done, was done.

Marketing men trade in hindsight: 20/20 vision, but blurred with a curtain of fear and disabled by a great blind-spot. Hindsight is perfect for covering your back; nobody takes the blame; if something worked before but does not work now, why, attribute it to blind caprice, malice, the whirligig of time bringing in his revenge. But it can show nothing of the future. A friend who has had dealings with Hollywood – an industry with a truly hierophantic attitude to the marketing cabbala – once said 'Marketing men are the ones who come up to you and say: "You know that truly extraordinary, original, innovative film you made? The one that broke all the rules? That nobody ever thought would succeed? That just came out of left field and broke all the records? Well... could you make another one, exactly the same?"'

> ## "Marketing men are the bogus priests and snake-oil men of modern commerce"

Marketing men dislike originality, virtue, idiosyncracy and commitment. They prefer the levelling tendencies of the plebiscite. A marketing man was once asked about the qualities which had given his company's lager supremacy in the market. 'It's not really that it has any particular qualities at all,' he said, with a candour rare in his trade. 'It's more that there's not really anything you can say against it.'

Thus, the gifts of the marketing men to our civilisation: blandness, imitation, predictability... and profound dishonesty. One of the nastiest diseases of our time is the belief that if you say something is so, it becomes so; this, too, is a marketing trick. The 'mission statement', the winsome rural label design, the tasteless cheese, the concept restaurant, the heritage theme park, the vernacular superstore: all these are the presents of marketing men to a country which knows it is being cheated but feels powerless to stop it. Blandness wrapped in mendacity: the prerogative of the marketing man through the ages.

Had there been a director of marketing at the Globe Theatre, can you believe that even one of Shakespeare's plays would have been staged as he wrote it?

Of course not. Because the one thing the marketing man cannot, literally, afford is to give offence. And so they end by offending us all.

MICHAEL BYWATER

PAY and DISPLAY CRECHE

1 hour £1.50
2 hours £2.50
3 hours £3.50
4 hours £4.50

Olden life

What was...
the Beastly Birthday Book?

IT WAS COMPILED by Nicolas Bentley, with pointed or rude remarks for each birthday boy or girl, drawn from classical authors, plus a few living ones, such as Shaw, Belloc, J B Morton (Beachcomber) and Aldous Huxley. Nicolas Bentley also drew the pictures.

Usually there are two quotations, the first intended for males, the second for females, each followed by a dotted line on which you signed your name. In practice, people would artfully pick the wrong one if they thought it the less beastly, i.e. less accurate. In my copy, a future television producer had nabbed, 'That ready wit may create many admirers but take my word for it, it makes few friends' (Lord Chesterfield), leaving the future wife of David Freeman no option but to settle for a sexist plonker from Lord Byron: 'To others' share let female errors fall / She had not even one – the worst of all'.

Evidently I acquired my copy second-hand or remaindered, because it was published (by Methuen) in 1934 while the earliest entries preserved in it date from 1943, my last term at school and first term at Cambridge on a Royal Engineers short course. Who can Betty Noyes have been, 'Whose heart was pure although her mind was shady' (W J Turner)? Ah, she was a bewitching student member of the London School of Economics, which had been evacuated to Cambridge, and briefly my girlfriend. Denis Gardner, who succeeded me in her affections and also got a rugger blue, has rather mysteriously opted for a clearly feminine second quotation – 'Can this be woman! Lovely and beloved!' (Matthew Gregory 'Monk' Lewis) – adding a manly 'No'.

A second stratum of entries dates from 1948, when I was at St Andrew's as an ex-service student. A third is circa 1979, when a daughter found the book in a box of old books in the loft and appropriated it. She, too, was just finishing school before going on to university, and an interesting thing about this generation of young persons is that they are much more casual about the BBB's rather ponderous assembly of ruderies. They ignore them, draw pictures over them or append sloppy messages. Having dutifully subscribed his name to a litany of abuse from George Borrow, one schoolmate adds plaintively, 'I am not horrid really'. The one or two striking bullseyes among the insults can be ascribed to the law of averages, I suppose. I hope that the eminent anthropologist Ian Whitaker, who came from Nottingham and cuts a commanding figure, won't mind being reminded of his draw (pictured left): 'The pear-shaped figure recalled that which is conventionally attached to the citizens of Nottingham' (Hilaire Belloc). As for the writer and pundit on sexual matters, William James, he should be well pleased with what he copped half a century ago from E C Bentley:

'Ought to have thought twice
About being a monster of vice.'

PHILIP PURSER

'Victor has those wonderful "gone to bed" eyes'

Nothing like a DAME

GILL McLAREN ROWE *recalls her year's engagement as personal assistant to*
DAME REBECCA WEST   **Illustration by PAUL HOGARTH**

It was through a friend of a friend that I came to be secretary/PA to Dame Rebecca West for a year or so from 1969. She had not been very worried when I confessed that I had read very little of her work. Her only comment had been, 'At least you're honest.' She also took it for granted that I could type, write shorthand and manage her accounts.

Dame Rebecca, or Dame Cecily Andrews, or Dame Cecily Fairfield, as she was variously known, had recently lost her husband, the merchant banker Henry Andrews. She had neither the will nor, I think, the wherewithal to continue living in Ibstone House in the Chilterns with its indoor and outdoor staff, and moved to a large, inconveniently laid out flat in Kingston House North, Princes Gate, not far from the Albert Hall. The flat was crammed with furniture from Ibstone House, a lifetime of priceless glass, china and cutlery from years of entertaining, and pictures – pictures covering every wall of every room, mostly originals and easily identifiable as Picassos, Dufys and other, older, artists. Dame Rebecca would proudly point out which were gifts from the artists and which she had 'acquired'. I think she had been good at 'acquiring' objects that caught her eye. The fireplace in the drawing-room was made of outstandingly beautiful eighteenth-century hand-painted porcelain, which she told me she had seen in a bombed house during the war and paid some men £5 to take out and carry away for her.

This amazing old lady lived her life exactly as it pleased her to. I would arrive at about 10am each day and let myself in, picking up the post. She was invariably still in bed with the newspapers, a tray of tea and a pair of scissors, industriously cutting out items of interest. She would call out as soon as she heard me, going straight into a conversation about what she was interested in and leaving me to pick up the thread as best I could. Although she kept an engagement diary it didn't mean much, since she would change her mind from hour to hour – but woe betide anyone who let her down! There was a telephone in every room, even the bathroom, and Dame Rebecca would wander from room to room, picking up the nearest telephone to call someone as the fancy took her and yelling at me to get off the line if I was in the middle of a call. While at home she would drink tea or coffee and eat biscuits without stopping, talking all the time and spitting out biscuit crumbs as she spoke. I soon got used to wiping out the mouthpiece when I used the phone.

Unless Dame Rebecca had a morning appointment she would take her time about getting up, having a bath, wandering around in her underwear and talking, talking, always talking. She walked with a curious rolling movement as both legs were swollen and her feet overlapped her shoes. Her hair had thinned with age and when anyone was expected, or she was going out, she would jam her wig on her head anyhow. I think it gave her a degree of confidence to feel it was there, although it looked no more natural than if she was wearing a hat. Her eyes were dark brown and deep set, and she saw a great deal more than many people realised until they read her books and articles. Her favourite scent was Hermès 'Calèche' which she used lavishly, sometimes sending passers-by reeling.

Dame Rebecca could be ruthless over what many people would not worry too much about. New curtains had been ordered for the drawing-room as she was not happy with those brought from Ibstone House. They were handmade from beautiful, gleaming, oyster-coloured silk, stiffened and lined to hang in precise folds, and so heavy that it took two men to lift each one. They had been sent back several times as Dame Rebecca found infinitesimal faults, but one day the men from the makers came to fit the poles and adjust the cords before the curtains were hung.

When the curtains were all in place – and the windows went round two sides of the drawing-room – the foreman demonstrated to Dame Rebecca how the cords worked, one to close them and one to open them, with a firm but gentle pull. Cutting the poor man short mid-explanation, she took hold of the first cord and yanked hard. Nothing happened and she yanked again. She had pulled the wrong cord and the effort she put into it pulled the pole off the bracket and the end of the curtain off the pole. Uttering one word, 'No!!!', Dame Rebecca walked out of the drawing-room, slamming the door. The workmen and I stood looking at each other until her voice was heard calling me from the study. She was on the telephone to the curtain company. 'Idiots, dolts, buffoons,' she was saying. 'Send me someone immediately who can do a proper job. And they can take the curtains away, they're ruined.'

Not many days went by without guests for luncheon, most of them well known. I remember the day the Muggeridges came. Both Malcolm and Dame Rebecca talked non-stop, neither listening to the other.

Although she could be kind and generous to people she liked (and who conformed to her ways), it was obvious that Dame Rebecca considered herself intellectually far superior to the majority of people around her. She had a number of friends, mostly widows like herself or sad elderly ladies who had never married, whom she managed for their own good. Some of them tried to stand up to her, but even they usually gave in for the sake of peace and quiet.

She decided eventually that she would go to New York and Mexico over Christmas 1969. I was to manage everything while she was away, and Augustina, the Spanish maid, would stay on to keep the flat clean. There was not a lot to do while Dame Rebecca was away. I arrived at the flat each morning, opened the post and, once her letters began to arrive, carried out her instructions. Augustina came each morning, vacuumed, dusted and polished like a whirling dervish. She was a little round dumpy figure dressed all in black apart from an old brown overcoat that looked like army surplus. She spoke only enough English to communicate with anyone on a very basic level and always said goodbye to me in Spanish while taking a holey pair

of woollen gloves out of her coat pocket and ramming her hands into them. She never carried a bag of any sort and stuck her hands in her pockets as I closed the front door after her.

In the New Year of 1970, I succumbed to the flu epidemic and had to stay at home for a week. I telephoned the head porter at Kingston House to tell Augustina that I was ill and she need not go in every day. She did not

She would drink tea and eat biscuits without stopping, talking all the time and spitting out crumbs

have a key, so a porter would let her into the flat and lock up after her.

About a week after Dame Rebecca's arrival home I arrived one morning to find her still in bed but surrounded by plastic bags full of necklaces – some valuable, and some downright tatty. She immediately demanded where a certain jade necklace was and I could only say I hadn't seen it. 'It's in one of the chests of drawers in one of the spare rooms,' she said, and then began a hunt through the spare bedrooms and the rooms in the maids' quarters, all crammed with furniture from Ibstone House. Dame Rebecca demanded the inventory for the contents of the flat, which turned out to be at her solicitors. I had not even known there was one, let alone seen it. However, her memory for her possessions was formidable and when we checked against the inventory we found an incredible amount of things missing, from jewellery to pictures, linen, china and glass, pots and pans and other sundry items. Naturally, the police were called and I felt completely responsible for the whole thing, although Dame Rebecca said she

didn't blame me. There was absolutely no sign of forced entry into the flat: as the only people who had keys apart from Dame Rebecca were the head porter and me, we both felt we were prime suspects.

Augustina had already been 'let go', as Dame Rebecca had decided she couldn't stand the sight of the small black figure around the place any longer. The police were interested to hear about her. When they went to her address they found an Aladdin's cave. All Dame Rebecca's possessions were there, crammed into the room in which she lived together with innumerable items from hotels where she had worked in the past, including a dozen brand-new rubber hot water bottles, hundreds of salt and pepper pots and piles of linen. Nothing she had taken had been sold. She was a compulsive kleptomaniac. I think she was eventually deported back to Spain, where she was also wanted by the police. But the mystery remains – how did she get even the small things out of the flat and past the porters, let alone large items such as pictures, when she never had so much as a shopping bag? The police found the old brown coat she always wore, suspecting at least poacher's pockets, but there was nothing.

Dame Rebecca gradually came to realise that it was very unlikely she would produce another book. She was old and tired and everything was becoming an effort. I left her each afternoon settled in the drawing-room with a tray of tea – and biscuits! – in front of the television watching *Crossroads*, which fascinated her.

I was sorry to leave, despite all the ups and downs, but we parted on good terms. From time to time she would telephone me 'just for a chat, my dear Gill' – the 'chat' turning into a monologue that went on for a very long time!

ORCHESTRAL
MANOEUVRES

Two years before his death in 1999 **YEHUDI MENUHIN** *talked to*
RICHARD INGRAMS *about his belief in the restorative powers of music*

When he was a boy Yehudi Menuhin had the conviction that if he played his violin well enough it would make everything better for everyone. 'I wanted to play Bach's great *Chaconne* for unaccompanied violin in the Sistine Chapel. I thought it would bring peace to the world.'

In the quiet, dark first-floor sitting-room of his house in Chester Square, Belgravia, the 81-year-old Menuhin (as always calm and serene despite a still-hectic schedule) admits with a smile that in retrospect it was rather a childish idea. 'Still, it had a grain of truth,' he adds. The point being that music, in his view, can not only bring comfort to the depressed but can help make us all better human beings. Everyone is musical, he insists. But not everyone is given the opportunity to respond at an early age to the power of music. It is this that has made him in recent years such a crusader for music in schools, and a campaigner for Susan Digby's Voices Foundation, which seeks to give singing a major role in the curriculum.

Ever an optimist with an apparently undentable faith in humanity, Menuhin frequently takes a pessimistic line these days. 'There are so many evils today,' he says. 'I think we are on the path to real catastrophe. Politically, economically, we seem to be thriving. But at the same time crime is rising. Certain schools have become schools for crime. It is in this area we believe that music, especially singing, can help. A child that sings, that child is not going to be a criminal.'

But what are they to sing? We have been joined by Diana, the beautiful former ballet dancer who has been at Menuhin's side through thick and

> **Music, in Menuhin's view, can not only bring comfort to the depressed but can help make us better human beings**

thin since their marriage in 1947. 'We always had hymn singing at school,' she says, in her decisive way. 'It was lovely, but they don't do that any more. And when I was a child 150 years ago every errand boy on his bicycle was whistling a tune. We had very good composers in those days like Cole Porter. Today everyone just pushes buttons.'

When she goes to her hairdresser, Lady Menuhin has to ask her coiffeuse to switch off the radio, 'For God's sake stop that irritating noise! It's so dismal. This is supposed to be a place of repose.' It is hard to imagine anyone daring to countermand her wishes.

But people no longer have the art of repose, says Menuhin. Silence is a vacuum that has to be filled, preferably with loud pop and rock. He once went to a Beatles concert and was appalled by the sheer volume of sound. 'Far too loud and far too distracting. I found it musically empty, deafeningly so. And the sight of millions of people sort of hypnotised by lights and the singers far away on the stage. It was so trite.'

At the same time, he feels, all is not well on the classical music front which is partly why he is talking about forming an orchestra of his own. 'Most of the performances of what we call classical music are not satisfactory. Even if the notes are right, notes are not sufficient. There is a real lack of style in playing today. It is rare to hear a really rousing, or a most beautiful performance of Mozart or Brahms. The players and conductor move from one imitation of a recording to another and put it together and say "That's the Brahms violin concerto".'

It is miles away from the approach of great artists of the past, like his friend the Spanish cellist Pablo Casals. 'Casals was very inspiring. He became another human being when he was playing. That creative element is missing now. We live in a reproductive age.' Menuhin always has in mind the one word which his first teacher Louis Persinger wrote on the score of the Beethoven violin concerto: 'Worship.' 'I never forgot it, whenever I played it, I saw that. Georges Enesco, my next teacher, when he sat at the piano or played the violin or conducted, it was service, it was dedication. The music came alive. It wasn't him that imposed the style. It wasn't him that said, "Look how marvellous I am! Look at the emotion I feel" – which is now so much the case. It was real authentic Mozart or Brahms that you were listening to. The passion, the intensity of deeply felt emotion.'

Still, Menuhin is the last person to give up on the crusade to 'make things better'. After a brush-off from the former education minister John Patten, he has now written to his Labour successor David Blunkett seeking a meeting to discuss music in schools. But can one hold out much hope of an audience for the world's greatest musician when the Prime Minister has recently fêted Noel Gallagher of Oasis as his guest of honour? To his eternal credit, Menuhin is the last person to be deterred by any such gloomy consideration.

'Is that you dear? What did you get as a leaving present?'

An Orthodox Voice
Demonic reality

IT IS REMARKABLE how few people today are prepared to talk about demons. There is willing belief in angels, and my American friends often tell me about UFO crashes, alien abductions and the infiltration of governments by malevolent space brothers. But if you inform them that most UFO phenomena are demonic or phantomesque, they have no idea what you are talking about. That is typical of the 'modern mind' that I keep complaining about. Having cast off the traditional myths and expressions, the modern mind is receptive to notions of any kind, however stupid and degraded. That is one form of demonic possession.

It is not that I truly believe in demons, or in anything else for that matter, but you can not deny Confucius, and he said that it is best to act as though such things existed. That is also what Patrick Harpur says in his book, *Daimonic Reality*, about recurrent types of unexplained phenomena. Its title refers to those daimones, named by the ancient Greeks as the causes of both good and bad luck and all kinds of weird happenings. Harpur suggests that this concept of a daimonic realm is the most effective way of coming to terms with the strangeness of our existence. You could call him a fairyland revivalist, but that would imply sentimentalism, and Harpur's stand for the traditional, aesthetic language of demonology against the space-fantasies created by the modern mind is impeccably reasoned. His account of the daimonic realm, its questionable attributes and its uncertain influence upon our lives, strikes me as more relevant to actual human experience than any modern work of science or psychology.

But then I wonder, do we really want demons back again, and all the spook paraphernalia that goes with them? In the old tales, Robin Goodfellow with his train of imps and elves was remembered with affection as merry though mischievous, but many people must have found him intolerable, for a great deal of effort was spent in exterminating him and his kind. The early Christians were engaged in perpetual war against demons, praying, chanting and ringing bells to expel them from their haunts. Church bells were invented as a powerful weapon for blasting away the local gods of paganism. An amusing poem of Chaucer describes the riff-raff preachers who infested the countryside and exorcised spirits in every house and corner. Women, he says, are now free from molestation by elves, but the old incubi have been replaced by the preachers themselves. It all came to the same thing, no doubt, but it is easy to see why respectable women of the Middle Ages might have preferred a young friar to some ancient rustic demon.

Yet, on the whole, I think Patrick Harpur is right and that demonology remains an essential part of the human syllabus. In no other terms is it possible to comprehend, for example, the recurrent, long-recorded phenomenon of animal mutilation, a demonic plague which is still very active in the western United States. How else can you sensibly regard yetis and Loch Ness monsters than as phantom products of another reality? Why bring in extra-terrestrials when every book of folklore tells you that elves and fairies are behind the abduction experience? It is not spacemen but the gods of good luck that sometimes lead me to the very book and page I need in the London Library. These creatures are everywhere because they occur naturally in our minds. If you do not call them demons you call them 'germs' or 'toxins', eat health foods and worry yourself to death on their account. You might as well recognise that the world is basically spiritual and adopt the appropriate terminology.

JOHN MICHELL

Those are PEARLS that were his EYES

An appreciation of Eric Ravilious
by RICHARD INGLEBY

From the series of submarine lithographs, 1941: main picture *The Commander*. Bottom, left to right: *The Diver*, *Off Watch*, *Men at Controls*

On 2nd September 1942 Captain Eric Ravilious RM, a thirty-nine-year-old painter working as a war artist for the Admiralty, climbed aboard an air reconnaissance craft flying out of Iceland and was never seen again. No debris was found, and although the 'missing' tag is a tragic one it seems somehow appropriate for a man whose paintings of the English landscape were often haunted by the absence of people and whose interiors always feel as if someone has just left the room.

> **Submarines were the subject of his most concerted body of war work: he revelled in their cramped conditions**

The world that Ravilious painted was well-ordered and carefully arranged, a mark of his training under Paul Nash in the design schools of the Royal College of Art in the early Twenties. The rigours of a design training stood him in good stead, but the most important lesson that Ravilious learnt from Nash was in the gentle art of watercolour painting – oil paints to Ravilious's way of thinking were too much like toothpaste.

Ravilious's paintings were more about mood than meaning, and that mood was a mix of melancholy and gentle humour. These days they seem to evoke the spirit of the Thirties – a nostalgic but entirely accurate vision of England between the wars.

People come and go in his pictures, but they are doll-like figures of little significance to the subject. The human content is more often evident by its absence – a coat on the back of an open door or a piece of abandoned farm machinery. The effect is haunting, occasionally menacing and sometimes slightly surreal, but is an accidental sort of surrealism found in the quirkiness of everyday life rather than a deliberate attempt by Ravilious to align himself to a modern movement. He belonged to a small band of English artists (his friend Edward Bawden was another) who understood the work of their more 'advanced' colleagues but had no personal interest in following them down the road to abstraction and into the mainstream of European Modernism.

The best of his watercolours date from the late Thirties, culminating in the summer of 1939 in a series of paintings depicting the ancient and peculiar figures that are cut into the chalk downs of southern England, but the outbreak of the Second World War brought the summer to an abrupt end.

Like his peacetime pictures, Ravilious's wartime work was under-stated, restrained in mood as well as colour, with no sign of the grandeur, nor heroism, nor the anger of war. He had always been drawn to machinery, enjoying its shape rather than its purpose, and the tools of war provided a catalogue of inspiring subjects. He was equally at home in the sinister world of submarines as with more simple subjects on dry land. As his friend Cecilia, Lady Semple, recalled, he had 'a burning desire to paint the Admiral's bicycle, but sadly found that the authorities wanted him to record something more warlike.'

Submarines were the subject of his most concerted body of war work – he revelled in their cramped conditions and what he described as 'the complexity of a Swiss clock'. The result was a series of ten lithographs and countless drawings. In July 1942 Ravilious requested permission to visit Iceland, a staging post for Atlantic convoys, 'to draw the Royal Marines with duffel coats and perhaps those splendid plum skies' and a few weeks later came the trip that was his last.

The English landscape has seldom looked so English as it did in Eric Ravilious's hands. As a watercolour painter he deserves his place alongside the likes of Turner, John Sell Cotman, Thomas Girtin and Francis Towner.

COUNTRY Life

RICHARD MABEY *contemplates the beautifully vicious nature of birds of prey*

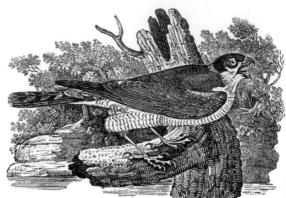

Sparrowhawk woodcut by Thomas Bewick, 1797

The garden stretched out like gardens should at midsummer, as lush and serene as a vicarage lawn. Fledgling blackbirds, deep in heavy-leafed shrubs, chinked monotonously. The comatose cats lay in the grass as placidly as Samson's lion. It was Eden before the Fall. Then out of the corner of my eye I glimpsed what appeared to be an enormous clockwork bird careering down the edge of the lawn. Its broad chocolate-brown wings whirred furiously, making me think for a moment it was a mallard crashing down from one of those rampant courtship flypasts. It was less than ten feet from my study window before I realised it was a female sparrowhawk that had just scooped up a young starling. The hawk stood stock-still on the grass, an awesomely beautiful bird with marbled chest feathers and a glittering gold eye. It clenched its talons tighter round the still-living starling, whose beak gaped open in pain and, no doubt, terror (hawks, contrary to belief, aren't always quick or clean killers), then flew off to finish the grisly business elsewhere.

This is the scene, enacted over increasing numbers of the nation's back gardens, which has made a curious common cause between suburban householders, gamekeepers and pigeon fanciers: piracy on the home patch; the slaughter of favourite small birds fondly stoked up with peanuts throughout the winter. Many who were appalled at the near extinction of birds of prey by agricultural pesticides are now outraged that their numbers have

recovered sufficiently for them to become garden raiders. The Duchess of Devonshire has famously described sparrowhawks as 'using a bird table like the Ritz bar', and campaigns to have them classed as vermin again.

> ## The hawk clenched its talons tighter round the still-living starling, whose beak gaped open in pain

I suppose I see a sparrowhawk kill in the garden once a year. Most of the time they pass rather casually overhead, spying out the land or enjoying the thermals. Only in wildlife documentaries are the lives of birds of prey given over single-mindedly to the chase. So the soft-hearted among us are spared frequent confrontation with the predator's imperative of killing – because that is what it does, neither mercifully nor cruelly, but necessarily. The red kites which have been so successfully introduced to the southern Chilterns are a case in point. They

are wonderfully adroit flyers, banking and wheeling like eagles one moment, then heading into the wind with wings shrunk back like falcons, and tilting their forked tails like rudders. But I have never seen one take so much as a worm, let alone a lump of carrion or a mouse. As in their flying, they seem to feed on air. At least hobby falcons do visibly eat.

A pack of six of these dashing falcons, with chestnut thighs and bandit moustachial patches, haunted our local reservoirs throughout May, scything among clouds of swifts, swallows and martins that congregate there in wet and windy weather. But this time the hobbies were only hunting daddy-long-legs and damsel-flies, for which of course not a single sentimental tear is shed. They skimmed over the water, turned cartwheels, stooped and stalled as they caught the flies with their feet. Then they would fly past more leisurely, holding the insect forward in one claw and munching it like an ice-cream cornet. In the autumn it's another matter, and the hobbies feast off the young swallows and martins that gather in thousands just before migration. It's a part of their lives that, as an occasional host to martins, I'm too squeamish to watch. But I console myself with the thought that neither hobbies, hawks, nor any other predators make any difference to the populations of their prey. If they did, they would, of course, wipe themselves out. An abundance of birds of prey, in garden or grouse-moor, is a kind of benediction, a sign that all's well with the habitat and its food chains.

East of Islington
The unusual life of Sam Taylor and friends

It's just not cricket

SAM TAYLOR *is made an offer she should have refused*

'I wondered,' he'd stumbled, 'if you might be interested in spending some time alone with me?' We had been strolling through the park, each attached to the leads of our respective pooches, when Willy's walker had decided to make his move. For the best part of a year now things had been just so. Darling Poopy had been allowing Willy, the frisky border terrier, to regularly cross the north/south divide from Chelsea and shower her with unconditional love and attention. Eventually, the sheer effort paid off.

Love had blossomed. Although not from the expected quarter. 'Umm,' he'd continued, 'I thought perhaps you might like to come to France, for, umm, a short holiday?' Admittedly, we had consumed several dinners together, and on occasion we had even been known to spend the odd weekend in the country, although only for the sake of the pooches, of course, but a holiday, in France, this was a radical new departure. He hadn't even met my father.

'Will we be completely alone?' I had replied. There was a long pause.

'Actually, no. There will be around eleven other people, although they won't be there all the time and we'll only have to see them during the day.' Why, I wondered, were there around eleven other people on this trip? What would they be doing there? And would we have anything in common? These earnest enquiries were met with a further pause, during which time my suitor squirmed and reflected on the failure of the English public school system to equip him to answer direct questions from women, while I reflected on the failure of *Cosmopolitan* magazine to reach those readers that need it most: English men.

Eventually, to put him out of his misery, I agreed to go. After all, my summer holiday alternatives were limited – so I opted for the romantic holiday

à deux (with eleven other people). After all, how bad could it really be?

Things started to go wrong at Dover. The boot was overhauled in a routine customs search. Willy's walker had been less than truthful with me. The boot of his newly cleaned, smart, sporty German automobile was full of the kind of contraband designed to send most sensitive women into a hysterical coma: it was full of cricket gear.

'What,' I screeched, 'are all those bats and balls doing mingling in among the *maillots de bain*?'

Another long silence.

'Are we on a cricket tour and you've failed to mention it?' I continued.

His flushed face stared, frozen, through the windscreen. Yes, it was indeed true, we were on a holiday of doom. We were on a cricket tour.

There are, it seems, certain rules which apply to females who get dragged along to cricket pitches. Even foreign pitches. First off, we get to sit on the sidelines. Secondly, we get to lay out the crockery and cutlery for tea. Thirdly, we get to clap and mutter words of congratulation and condolence when something happens on the great green yonder. As all girls are trained to perform the first two tasks from birth, these are not so difficult to follow. It's the third task that can prove the most tricky.

Nothing, but nothing, happens at a cricket match that can be deemed of any interest to any woman who still has a firm grasp of her faculties. Occasionally, a middle-aged man gets injured attempting the kind of flying manoeuvre that once forced Nadia Comaneci to retire from international gymnastics, while the other players stand around muttering something about silly legs – but mostly nothing happens.

And then they have tea. In Bordeaux they had tea. In Saumur they had tea. In fact, wherever we went they had tea and mumbled to each other about the position and condition of their silly legs. But mostly they drank tea. At the end of the games they awarded each other cups – the French hosts heartily thanking the British visitors for travelling all that way to take tea with them and the British visitors roundly applauding the size and magnitude of the teas provided, and so it went on, all over France.

On the last night of our romantic holiday *à deux* (with eleven other people), Willy's walker took me to an incredibly expensive, chic, romantic restaurant. I sensed that he had been itching to ask me something all day. Perhaps this was it. Perhaps the French air had got to him and he was about to pop the question. Perhaps this was why he had brought me on this romantic holiday *à deux* (with eleven other people). I was suddenly in a blind panic. How will it affect Poopy? Should I say yes or no? Unable to contain himself any longer, he leaned over the candlelit table, lowered his eyes and spoke:

'Darling?'

'Yes?' I smiled back nervously.

'Can I ask you something?'

'Please do,' I urged.

'I don't suppose that you noticed that I took the best catch of my life this afternoon, did you?'

The answer was definitely no.

ILLUSTRATION: PETER BAILEY

OLD BOYS

You can't always guess what will happen to your classmates or how far they might go. **WILLIAM TREVOR** *remembers one nondescript youth who confounded all expectation*

Mak Choon Moon has gone back to Kuala Lumpur; Ridgeway, PLK, is rearing ostriches for meat. D K Fisher (1960) harnesses the wind, B J Lansdale (1956) is a Justice of the Peace. Southgate, WME, has joined the family business. H K McKeever (1984) has assisted in the construction of a dam.

Once a year the Old Boys Bulletin comes, listing the subscribers to the last Appeal, bringing the news from Sligo and County Clare and Cork, from Fakenham and Yeovil, from New South Wales and Chile and Moldavia. T M Hopking (1951) has left the tea industry, de Courcy-Hartley is running a hotel. The Reverend J R Sheill (1931) has retired to Youghal, having always loved the sea. C C Roe (1949) writes from Kenya and would welcome visitors.

Is J M Kingsmill Moore (1942) the Kingsmill Moore who was in love with Ingrid Bergman for the whole of an Easter term after seeing *For Whom the Bell Tolls?* Is D C L Jameson (1941), now a Canon of the Church of Ireland, the Jameson who was a clever scrum-half though sometimes slow to pass the ball? Not to be confused with Popeye Jameson of the whiskey family, who was so unjustly expelled? Whatever became of old

Popeye? Whatever became of Stuffy Malone, and John Kane Archer in his bookmaker's tweeds? And Poodle Tennyson, and the temporary master who rifled the changing-room lockers? And the Byng brothers – long before my time – reputed to have disturbed a grave in the Moravian cemetery beyond the golf-course to see if the Moravians were buried standing up? I G Sainsbury has died. 'You wrote a poem,' Earle reminded me one teatime, a fact he should not have known, since all contributions to the school's alternative magazine were submitted on the understanding that there was confidentiality. Not meaning to hurt, since he was not that kind of boy, Earle said he knew about the poem because Sainsbury – editor of the alternative magazine – had lit his cigarette with it in the Printing Club. Handsome and stage-struck, Earle died too, a long time ago on a tour of Africa, still funny in *Present Laughter*, the first of my friends to go.

Now they go all the time, age being what it is. The Marriages column, and the Births, once interesting, are less so as the years pile up. Could this Odlum – R T G, 1973 – be the son of the Odlum I knew so well? Is the Goodbody of 1967 possibly related to the Goodbody who made inept fags wash the common-room dishes all over again if traces of egg remained on a plate? At one remove too many, such speculations flop limply, before the page is turned.

A few years ago a name sprang out from among the Deaths. Easy to forget, this boy, difficult to place. No Widmerpool, no attractive Stringham, no daring Templer. Not even in minor ways defying the school uniform – the knot of his plain grey Stackallan house tie neither too loose nor too tight in its soft grey regulation collar – hair sleeked, apologetic face, he blended so easily with the mass that his unobtrusiveness seems now like art. He would, perhaps some of us imagined, one day take pride in a Clark Gable moustache, something to cheer those slightly empty features. A watch-chain dangling from a lapel, brown suit and all the buttons of a waistcoat buttoned: for an instant there might have been such an image, filched from a distant middle age.

Something prevents me from naming this boy. There is a privacy to be observed, although in the Bulletin, of course, his identity was clearly stated, and his year of entry. He lived near Monasterevin in County Kildare, a tidy house by the roadside in the country. My father and I used to pick him up at the beginning of term, for although petrol was practically non-existent in Ireland during the war ('the Emergency', as we called it), my father always seemed to be able to lay his hands on some. A battered green trunk was carried from the tidy house, no tuck-box.

'Good holidays?' my father would enquire and be politely told that yes, the holidays had been good. And my father would say something else and be answered, and that for the remainder of the journey would be that. Years afterwards it was the green trunk, not the boy, that my father remembered.

Disliked by no one, argument or contradiction not his way, the boy we gave a lift to drifted through one term and then another, smiling when a smile was called for by some waggish master, kneeling in Chapel with an upright back, as the requirement was. Neat, ordinary handwriting filled a page with details of Caesar's Gallic War, and listed on another New Zealand's resources. Friendships were mild, no passion there. Never a frequenter of smokers' lairs, not one to find his way to the cupboard where the communion wine was kept, not one to confess outrageously to Brother Charles when once a year he visited, this boy was somehow not a goody-goody: being that would have been to give himself airs. Photography was his hobby – patient photographs of hills and flights of birds.

'He'll come to a sticky end,' we predicted about Piggott-Browne or Anselm. Neither did, in fact, the first rising to great heights in packaging, the second still distinguished in academe. We liked to spot the sticky ends, often seeing ourselves among them. Others we saw as army men and businessmen, solicitors and surgeons

> ## We liked to spot the sticky ends, often seeing ourselves among them. Others we saw as army men and businessmen, solicitors and surgeons and engineers, architects and farmers, painters and journalists

and engineers, architects and farmers, painters and journalists. Accountancy we probably guessed for the boys whom no one disliked, if we bothered to guess anything at all.

Perhaps it was because people forgot he was there that he outdid us all in the end. The Bulletin was circumspect, naturally not reporting that he died in jail, that years before he had released the handbrake and jumped, had stood and watched and heard the screams, as in an old Hollywood film. When a few of us meet now the name bewilders, the face has gone until we drag it back. 'Not the one who'd eat your swedes?' 'Not Colville, who sang in his sleep?' No, not Colville, nor the one who'd finish your turnips for you, although he might have. 'There were initials on that trunk,' my father said when I told him. He had read about the case, he said. Something went wrong. The corpse was found in a bog, not where it should have been, the grisly story goes. There was no doubt about the guilt, the awful act so clumsily performed that the truth stared the police and judge and jury in the face. Yet he was never one for that – for clumsiness, for murder. You'd swear on oath he wasn't.

I have not been back to look, but in the old school groups that one after another stretch for miles, it seems, on the dark panelling outside the Dining Hall I'm told he's quietly still there. A presence not at all like that of Sealy minor, who manages in his gifted way to appear twice in the same photograph. Kingston has tied his house tie into a bow, Fitzmaurice has turned his back. But taking it all seriously, neat in every detail, the boy we took for granted smiles his polite smile.

'Good day, may I speak to the gingerbread man of the house?'

NOT MANY DEAD

Important stories you may have missed

Firefighters have rescued an array of hedgehogs from a vertical drainpipe. The crew from Humberside Fire and Rescue Service used barbecue tongs to retrieve the animals from the pipe in Burbage Avenue.
Hull Daily Mail

A new grit bin at Keddington Road in Louth will not be provided this winter.
Horncastle Target

Detectives who retrieved a headless corpse from a river summoned a doctor to confirm he was dead, an inquest heard.
Evening Standard

There has been a small earthquake in Cumbria. No one was hurt.
BBC Radio 4 News

A marmalade produced by Environment Minister Lord Henley has won the top prize at the World Marmalade Awards.
Independent

A confused resident called out fire crews after mistakenly thinking there was someone trapped under his sofa.
East Anglian Daily Times

MEMORY LANE

A Narrow Escape
JOHN RYAN

SEEING A PICTURE of Mussolini's motorcar vividly brought back to me an episode from my schooldays. I was seventeen, the year was 1938. My father was British Minister in Albania, and I was spending the Easter holidays there.

My return to school via Rome coincided with Hitler's visit to Mussolini. My brother and I were to stay a few days with our Air Attaché in Rome and, filled with the fashionable left-wing radicalism of those times, I had the idea of seeing whether I would get an opportunity to assassinate the two Fascist leaders. To pursue this fantasy further I had to assume that I would be able to procure a small bomb in Albania – this, had I really tried to do so, might well have been possible. In place of the putative 'bomb', however, I bought a heavy tin of halva, a delicious sweetmeat from those parts, and this, a cylindrical tin about three inches by four, I thought of henceforth as my weapon.

In the first place it had to be brought into Italy. Here was no problem. There was no baggage examination at the port of Bari. In Rome therefore, with the 'bomb' now concealed in my box camera (as I pretended), it was a question of whether the opportunity would arise to deliver it.

When Hitler arrived at the station in Rome he was welcomed with barbaric splendour which I have never forgotten. It was evening, and the two leaders drove together down a wide avenue flanked by huge blazing torches thirty feet high. Armed with my camera, my brother and I took up our places early in the front rank of spectators. Nobody examined my camera, but by the time the

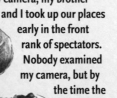

procession passed we had been pushed back and back by ranks of troops, Blackshirt militia and security guards. Sixteen rows from the front we watched as party officials moved among the crowd distributing Nazi flags and instructing the people to shout 'Hitler! Hitler!' as the great men passed. There was no chance at that range to throw my 'bomb'.

Next day, however, Hitler and Mussolini were due to lay wreaths on the great Vittorio Emmanuale Memorial. Their route lay through the Piazza Venezia and we, privileged guests of our Air Attaché, had seats on a first-floor balcony overlooking the Piazza. Would anybody, I wondered, examine the camera which I carefully slung over my shoulder? Nobody did.

The great Piazza was an astonishing sight. The whole centre was packed with troops in close formation. With their round helmets they reminded me of a huge set of closely packed ball-bearings.

Then the motorcade arrived, and I watched Hitler and Mussolini, side by side, pass a mere twenty feet beneath me. My 'bomb', had I had one and had I thrown it, could not have missed. And there my fantasy ended. The motorcade passed, the leaders did their stuff on the steps of the Memorial, and that was that. My chief recollection is of the peculiarly nasty colour of Hitler's brown uniform.

And had I really had the bomb – so easily brought to the right spot at the right time – and had I thrown it, would the course of history have been changed? Very possibly not. It was widely rumoured that the public appearances of the dictators were in fact those of doubles. In which case the only one whose history would have been altered would have been mine.

In the years since the war I have come to know Italy well. Italians seem wonderfully opposed to any form of regimentation. How they ever came to fall under the Fascist sway remains a complete mystery. Thank heavens that is all over now... we hope.

The world according to
Enfield Snr

And the winner of the Billingshurst Brewery Prize is...

Readers may be interested to know of the establishment of the Billingshurst Brewery Prize for the silliest remark of the year. There is, as it happens, no Billingshurst Brewery, but I do not see this as an obstacle. The title sounds well, and I do not suppose that the Whitbread judges were, if you will forgive the vulgarism, merely there for the beer. To help me in my deliberations a panel of judges of astonishing capacity has been invited, consisting of Jerry Hall, Naomi Campbell, Catherine Zeta Jones and Elizabeth Hurley. Unfortunately I was the only one able to get to our first meeting, but this had the result that the discussions were amicable and the decisions unanimous.

The year is young but the competition is already hot. We thought Mrs Posh Spice made a good try with: 'It did worry me because I started to get paranoid', but we felt this should perhaps be treated as a slip of the tongue (or *lapsus linguae*, as Miss Jones would have called it, the Welsh being rather good at Latin). Laura Zachary of the Ski Club of Great Britain did well with: 'At the end of the day it is a personal decision whether to ski "off".' At the end of the day it is dark, and to ski off-piste in the dark must surely be a silly idea, but the words are somehow lacking in that weight and density which characterises a really obtuse remark.

No such objection can be made to: 'A free vote would be a concession to bigotry', from Alice Mahon, Labour MP for Halifax. This has a laconic simplicity which sets off its stupidity to perfection, but unfortunately there is a doubt as to her exact words. The paper describes her as 'denouncing a free vote as a concession to bigotry', but that might just have been the general tenor of her remarks, without the lapidary phrase that I have quoted. We therefore reluctantly scratched her from the competition.

We spent some time on Professor Hugh Pennington and his: 'I think I would go to the extreme of saying that perhaps it is unwise to take a five-year-old or under on a farm visit, because we have had such serious complications in the very small number of kids who've been infected.' This scores highly on pomposity, hesitancy and general obfuscation. Professor Pennington seems to be saying: 'As there have been serious complications (by which I mean illness) in a very small number of young goats, I think (but am not yet decided) that I would (but might not) go to the extreme (though I might perhaps stop short) of saying that perhaps (but perhaps not) it is unwise (but no more than unwise) to take a child under six to a farm' – presumably a farm where there are young goats. In the end we decided there might be a grain of sense in this somewhere, and anyway it could not stand up against a glorious offering from Polly Toynbee. 'Turn to the dictionary of quotations,' she says, 'and there is barely a reference to England and the English that doesn't make you blush.' 'Let the experiment be made,' we cried with one voice (mine; Miss Jones would have said '*Fiat experimentum*') and turned to the *Oxford Dictionary of Quotations*. It was at once revealed that this is serious, heavyweight nonsense. Of some 140 appropriate references, about a third are non-starters, as I don't see why phrases like 'Ireland gives England her soldiers' should bring a blush to the Toynbee cheek. Another third are of a humorous or derogatory nature, and I would think she could keep her countenance when told that England is a nation of shopkeepers. The rest can, on a very wide definition, be regarded as patriotic.

Now I am ready to believe that anything that smacks of patriotism is repugnant to Ms Toynbee. She may have a deep aversion to Blake, Brooke, Browning and Kipling; a dislike of Wordsworth and a horror of Shakespeare. John of Gaunt's speech may turn her puce and she may emerge from a performance of *Henry V* looking like a beetroot. She may, but she has no business to suppose that the rest of us are half so daft. Indeed, I do believe that even she had only to glance at the work of reference to which she refers to see that what she was about to write was the merest nonsense. But she didn't, which is why we like her contribution so much, as a classic application of the rule: 'Never seek to establish the facts as they may disturb your settled prejudices.'

'I'll be honest with you, Mrs Gribswell – the signs are not good'

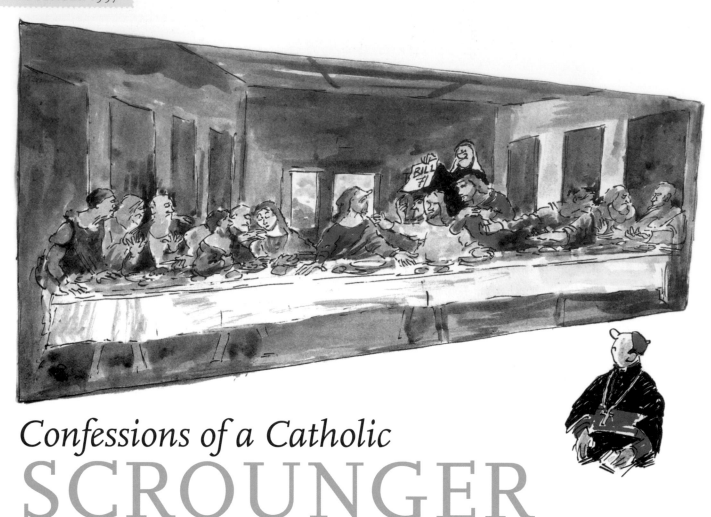

Confessions of a Catholic
SCROUNGER

Why I am persona non grata at retreat houses everywhere, by **WILFRED DE'ATH**

Illustrations by LARRY

Recently I decided to make a short Catholic retreat, and it was arranged that I should spend a day or two with the sisters of Jeanne Delanoue, Mother of the Poor, at their *maison mère* in St Hilaire-St Florent, just outside Saumur. After about four days there I felt so much better than I had in twenty years of retreat-going that I felt like leaving the good sisters some money. I didn't, of course, because I didn't have any, and anyway they didn't expect it, but the thought was there, at least.

In 1978 I spent an entire month with the Community of the Resurrection in Mirfield, Yorkshire, trying to decide whether or not to become a Roman Catholic (Mirfield, in fact, is very High Anglican). They had a guest-master who, far from making his guests feel welcome, always seemed glad to see the back of them. I shall never forget the look of smug satisfaction on his face as the taxi swept a departing guest away. This increased as he examined the large cheque the guest had left behind. I resolved to pay as little as possible for my stay and, in fact, gave him only £20 for the whole month. For many years after that Father Luke wrote to me

regularly saying that I should 'not lose sight of' the money I still owed them.

I have always understood the principle of monastic hospitality to be that you treat your guest as though he were Jesus Christ come to stay for a while, and you certainly wouldn't dream of shoving a bill on Our Blessed Lord's breakfast plate within a few days of his arrival. But that is what increasingly happens in convents and monasteries these days.

They did try to maintain the monastic principle at Douai Abbey (Benedictines) where I often used to go on retreat after becoming RC. They never seemed to ask for, or expect, any money, so I would occasionally drop a fiver into the collection plate at Mass on Sunday, if I could afford it – or even if I couldn't. But even Douai, the most tolerant of places, got fed-up with my free-loading. The Prior, who disliked me, caught me making a long-distance phone

The Abbot Washing the Guests' Feet

DETAIL

call to France and I became *persona non grata* after that. I understood why, of course, but I still maintain that in the strictest sense they were wrong to exclude me from their peaceful, religious life.

I used to go to Worth Abbey (also Benedictines) after that, where the Abbot put a full bottle of Scotch on the table of an evening and proclaimed that neither of us would make a move towards bed until it was empty. Neither of us did. Then I went to the snobbish Downside where the double-barrelled Bursar tried to institute criminal proceedings against me for bouncing a cheque on their bookshop. Downside is one of the richest monasteries in the world, presiding over 500 acres of rich farmland and an extremely expensive public school, they eat eight courses at dinner on Feast Days, yet they seem unable to accommodate a poor NFA (No Fixed Abode) like me even for a few days.

For some years I became the scourge of retreat houses all over England, leaving a trail of distraught guest-masters behind me. The Prior at Boar's Hill, Oxford (discalced Carmelites), still has a nervous breakdown when my name is mentioned, since I found a way of sneaking in to stay at the Priory for days at a time without informing anyone of my presence. I think they got angry because my presence in their midst underlined the essential hypocrisy of their position in respect of hospitality, epitomised for me (at Douai, I'm afraid) when we sang the psalm, 'And let me never forget my poorer brother' at midday office, and then watched the Prior see off a group of tramps who had gathered at the refectory door in search of nourishment. I suppose my own behaviour was a kind of tacit revenge, a way of saying that you can't have it both ways.

The only retreat house in the UK where I am still *persona grata* is, oddly, not a Catholic one at all, but a Charismatic one, Fursey House in the New Forest, where they let me stay for several weeks without payment as recently as 1996. Money was never mentioned so, of course, I felt like paying. (*But did you?* No.)

Things are not much better here in France where I have been 'retreating' since 1991. The first I ever went on was with some very weird nuns at a place

THE SCROUNGER PARTING WITH HIS FIVER.

THE GOOD SAMARITAN

called Beaufort, in a remote part of Brittany. Their liturgy included dancing around the altar at vespers and strange incantations at compline. It was all a shade eerie. I left them 200 francs, all I had on me, but the Prioress, who was a cripple, stamped her club-foot with rage and threatened me with the police. I don't think I shall be going back.

In 1992, I went to Solesmes, the great Benedictine Abbey in the Somme (160 monks), where the Abbot washes the hands and feet of each guest on his first evening. He welcomed me as 'an old Oxfordian' and said I might stay as long as I wished. I would have done so except that the *vin de table* they served at dinner tasted like red ink and gave me an upset stomach. I went back in 1994 but they had got wise to me by then and, after a few days, demanded *un petit cadeau*, i.e. money (precisely the term used by prostitutes in France). Also, the assistant guest-master, an American, was a raving queer who wouldn't stop dropping in to see me to discuss the state of my soul. So I got fed up and left. But I miss all those monks doing their Gregorian Chant.

In Lourdes I stayed with the nuns at St Joseph's Convent. While I was there, someone broke in and desecrated their chapel and stole two thousand francs. I was the suspect, so the nuns called in a Clouseau-like inspector who threatened to throw me into a bare cell, strip me naked and 'beat the living shit' out of me. In the end, he had to let me go for lack of evidence.

In October 1995 I stayed for a week at the famous Taizé Community in Burgundy. I slept in a broken bed in a room with no light bulb or washing facilities, sharing with an elderly German. We ate disgusting food in a broken-down tent, like refugees in a war zone. For this they wanted £100 a week! When I complained to Frère Roger, aged 82, a friend of the Pope and of the late Mother Teresa, he seemed quite startled. 'No one has ever complained before,' he said. 'You do not understand our difficulties here.'

I understood them only too well. Their difficulty is getting gullible guests to pay through the nose to live in conditions you wouldn't keep a dog in. And all in the name of Christianity. Taizé was a kind of Christian concentration camp, where you were refused even a cup of cold water.

I've only once, in twenty years, felt guilty about not paying for a retreat, and that was when I stayed with some Spanish sisters in Lourdes in December 1992. They really did seem poor, and I think they genuinely needed money. They belonged to an order called Sisters of the Love of God and, as I pointed out to their superior, that very title implied – to me, at any rate – that they must occasionally accommodate someone like myself for nothing. She seemed to see my point and, when she did so, I at once felt like paying her. And one day I shall.

More than a man can BEAR

It's cold as hell, tough guys eat squirrels and parrots are forbidden to speak in English. No wonder **MORDECAI RICHLER** *prefers London to Quebec in the winter*

Strangers, who obviously take me for an imbecile, ask again and again: 'You mean to say you come to London for the winter months?' Yes I do. Born and bred in Montreal, I have, all the same, long looked on London as my second home. I first sailed for England on the *Franconia* in 1950, my intended short stay broken up by lengthy sojourns on the Continent, extending to more than twenty years. I met my wife in London and four of our five children were born here. We returned to Canada in 1972. In 1993, our children grown up, Florence and I acquired a flat in SW3, which we have made our winter quarters.

Natives of this island who regard our choice as bizarre are happily unaware of the alternative. Six months of punishing winter. Icy streets. Frozen pipes. Cars that won't start. Three-day blizzards. Never mind this winter's Great Ice Storm, which paralysed Mon-

treal for ten days, leaving it without light or heat. It is also good to escape Quebec's loopy language laws. Among other petty-minded strictures, the French Language Charter, which was introduced by our separatist provincial

> **Natives of this island who regard our choice as bizarre are happily unaware of the alternative**

government in 1977, prohibits English on outdoor commercial signs, unless the English lettering is half the size of the French. In the absence of Keystone Cops, this is enforced by our language police – or tongue-troopers as they have been dubbed – armed with tape measures. Pondering corruptions of the language of Racine, Voltaire and

Brigitte Bardot, alert Québécois lexicographers have legislated the humble 'hamburger' edible by renaming it the 'hambourgeois'.

In the spring of 1996 an alert inspector from the Office de la Langue Française was responsible for what became celebrated as 'the Matzoh Bust'. Weeks before Passover he espied boxes of imported matzohs, labelled in English only, on the shelves of a kosher grocery in Montreal, and ordered them removed. The story, a real knee-slapper, was carried round the world, embarrassing Quebecers. So the government had second thoughts. It exempted matzohs from French labelling regulations for forty days before Passover and twenty days after. Those Jewish felons who, like me, might fancy a delicious matzoh omelette on the illegal 68th day have the satisfaction of knowing that we are bonding with the *conversos* of fifteenth-century Spain, who also had to practise their religious rites in secret.

No sooner was the matzoh crisis settled than another francophone zealot struck. An indignant customer of a Montreal pet shop threatened to complain to the Commission de Protection de la Langue Française, because a parrot called Peekaboo spoke English only.

Our separatist Parti Québécois government has succeeded in dividing Quebecers into the *pure laine* and *les autres*, that is to say the pure and impure woollies. The former is composed of old-stock francophones, the overwhelming majority, and the latter of anglophones and so-called allophones (Italians, Greeks, Portuguese, and so on). I'm proud to report that Quebec's Jews, most of us descended from East European *shtetls*, pass muster as anglophones, even as we are incongruously dubbed 'Anglo-Saxon Jews' in Israel.

The French Language Charter's ultimate goal is to make French the common language of all Quebecers. So, understandably, alarm bells went off when a government report revealed that sneaky impure woollies still read English-language newspapers and magazines, sometimes even books, and watched English-language TV and videos at home. Worse news. There was damning evidence that the ungrateful children of allophone immigrants, who were obliged to attend French-language schools, preferred to flirt in English in their schoolyards.

I would be remiss if I suggested that all francophone Quebecers were intolerant of anglophones. Or were intimidated by anglophone royalty for that matter. Take, for instance, the case of pop singer Charlesbois, a Québécois *vedette*. It has been reported that, seated

next to the Duchess of York at a dinner party last year, he said: 'It has to be easy for the Queen to go to the hairdresser.'

'I don't understand,' said Fergie.

'She just has to point to a stamp, or her picture on a £20 note, and say "I want it done like that".'

Neither would it be fair to suggest that life is a misery for an English-speaking novelist in *la belle province*. I enjoy a certain frisson, scribbling in a language that affronts Quebec's *visage linguistique*.

Until 1993, Florence and I saw out the long winters rooted in our dacha on the shores of Lake Memphremagog, in Quebec's Eastern Townships, hard by the Vermont border. Giving up the Townships for London has deprived us of a number of social-cum-cultural events, among them the annual Wild Game Dinner at The Owl's Nest, an unassuming watering hole perched on cinder blocks out on Highway 242.

The Owl's Nest banquet is not for vegans. Tables are laden with wild turkey. Deer livers sizzle in pans, while porcupine, grey squirrel and black bear

bubble in cauldrons (coyote is eschewed for being too chewy). The delicacies are washed down with quarts of Molson's Ex and a brand of Ontario *vino* that could, in a pinch, clear car windshields of frost. Smoking, bawdy language and sexual harassment are encouraged, but 'wacky-baccy' is not tolerated. In the absence of a string quartet, the management provides a fiddler, screechy beyond compare, or somebody who can master the battered piano with the six missing keys. This long, enchanted evening usually culminates in one of the celebrants breaking a chair over the head of a neighbour, his hollered explanation charged with baffling sexual contradictions, as in, 'You've been screwing my woman, you fucken little faggot'.

Among my good companions in the Townships I count Big Foot. Big Foot winters in a remote cabin high in the hills, but once a week he descends through the snow drifts to The Hooter, another bar on the 242. Attired in a shiny black suit and soiled white shirt with a ruffled collar, sporting an enormous bejewelled crucifix in place of a necktie, he will sit down at a table and order three quarts of Molson's. Then he will bet anybody a dollar that he can lift him off the floor by his trouser belt 'wiff my teef'. One week Big Foot did not appear at The Hooter, so a bunch of regulars piled into a four-wheel drive, laden with cases of beer, and headed for the hills. A distraught Big Foot was discovered staring into space at his kitchen table. 'My wife must be very angry wiff me,' he said. 'She hasn't spoken to me for two nights. I can't get her out of bed.'

One of the regulars went into the bedroom and returned to tell Big Foot: 'She ain't angry with you. She's dead.'

'Oh, so that's it,' said Big Foot, enormously relieved.

'What did you say Albert was taking for his asthma?'

In bed with *Raven*

SIMON RAVEN, *the novelist, dramatist, memoirist, critic, gambler and epicurean, in conversation with* **NAIM ATTALLAH.** *Portrait by* **JANE BOWN**

I have the impression that your passion for the classics and your respect for the teaching of the Ancients has shielded you to some extent against the realities of the modern world. Would you agree?

They have certainly shielded me against a lot of nonsense that is spoken in the modern world. Both the Greeks and the Romans were full of direct and pithily expressed commonsense, much of which would be considered unacceptable today. Also the study of the classics is a very absorbing matter, involving quite a lot of concentration and hard work, which in itself shields one from all the follies going on outside. I hardly ever read a newspaper these days except for the racing sections. Newspapers contain so much sentimental rubbish and self-pitying whining about this and that, rape and murder, or photos of politicians in silly positions sucking up to rows of proletarian children. I just don't have time for that. The trouble with this is that when the modern world does break through, which it is bound to do from time to time, it is uniquely unpleasant.

In your book, *An English Gentleman*, you say that by becoming a writer one bade farewell at once to ethical restraint and to any kind of conventional status in society. Have those two factors been the cornerstones of your writing?

They were advantages that came with the trade. The point I was trying to make was that if one was a regular army man, or a don, or a schoolmaster, or a Foreign Office man, one had to observe the code, largely a Christian code – and this still applies. Writers did not have to observe a code, and I was very grateful for this.

You say that you don't expect your novels to be remembered. Is this something you regret?

I would very much like some of my work to be remembered, but when I consider what has happened to better novelists in my own lifetime, it's extremely unlikely that my own work will last. If you take a novelist such as Francis Brett Young, who was very important in my parents' day – whoever hears of him now? It seems to me that in order to be remembered as a novelist you have to be of supreme merit and also enjoy a lot of luck. I could still hope in a corner of my mind not to be forgotten, but the omens are not good.

In an article in the *Listener* in 1962 you gave an account of your addiction to gambling in which you spoke of 'the treasury of terror, guilt and perversity' which it entailed. You suggested that the principal motive for gambling in your case was the desire to be punished when things went badly, and the 'almost sexual satisfaction' to be derived from an evening of disastrous losses.

If it is indeed sexual, it is surely masochistic...

Yes, I think it is. It is quite true that all those things accompanied my gambling, and there was definite sexual excitement. That is partly to do with fear, I think. I can remember when I was a very young boy doing a long division sum for an exam and I couldn't get it to work out. Time went on and I had no time left for other questions, and I found myself becoming distinctly sexually aroused. I also remember getting a huge erection underneath one of Aspinall's gambling tables when I was still allowed to go there.

I now see that the only form of gambling which is really amusing is horse racing. You can't hope to win at horse racing because you don't know how the horse feels. That's why hot favourites lose to 33-1 numbers, and a wail of self-pity goes up from the crowd. It's my favourite thing, particularly if I've backed the 33-1 number. The point about horse racing is that it is just fun, it's an exciting sporting spectacle, you don't know what is going to happen, the colours are beautiful, the band plays, there are blue hills in the background, and so it becomes almost a cultural obligation to go to the horse races. Toulouse Lautrec and Degas knew this, as did lots of fine artists.

When you were at prep school you were a victim of sexual abuse at the hands of the games master. You obviously didn't see yourself as a victim; indeed you felt what you called 'great erotic fascination' with what went on. Is that how you choose to remember it, or do you think that is how it actually felt at the time?

It's certainly how I choose to remember it, and I think it actually felt that way at the time. One knew, of course, that there was something not quite right about it, but what made it feel more right than it possibly was, was the fact that Colonel K, as I call him, was a very good schoolmaster, a very charming man, kind, pleasant, and representing the best of the prep school system. He taught mathematics, English literature and geography with imagination and esprit. And as regards sex, what he did was very pleasant, no two ways about it. Small children can be sexually excited, and certainly by the time I was nine or ten I was having a sort of orgasm, and the whole business was very enjoyable. He played with the other boys too, and we all did it to each other, and also to him. And great fun it was too.

I think I'm right in saying that you regarded yourself as bisexual, which, in the 1950s, was not exactly fashionable. Did you ever wish that you were one thing or the other, so to speak?

No, I've been very happy being bisexual. It seemed to me the intelligent and civilised solution. It was the position taken up by all my favourite classical authors, and a lot of my favourite more modern authors, who, even if they themselves weren't bisexual, certainly condoned the condition and sometimes actively approved it. It's so matchlessly convenient to be able to help yourself either way if the opportunity presents.

You have a reputation for misogyny. Does it have a rational basis? You obviously have strong feelings about the worthlessness of women, their 'inability to act sensibly', as you put it.

These answers are not to be oversimplified. Like everybody else I've had a lot of experience of the foolishness of women, and the foolishness of men too. On the one hand, men tend to be sexually vain and greedy. Women, on the other hand, tend to be possessive and domestic. This is quite simply biological, since nature tells us that women are there to have babies; they are naturally possessive of men so that a family can be formed. This can make them in any number of ways very tiresome. They don't want their husbands to go out on a drunken evening or do jolly things like racing, because that uses up money which is meant for babies. I find this aspect of women particularly tedious.

Also this business of wanting to be in on male things. Women have gone to endless trouble to penetrate male clubs. Well, if they want clubs, why can't they have their own? After all, it's very good for people to be able to get away from the opposite sex, for women as well as men.

While you were at King's it came as a shock when your girlfriend Susan Kilner announced she was pregnant. The prospect of marriage appalled you, yet you caved in under pressure 'to do the decent thing'. Was this not uncharacteristic behaviour – I mean, to do what was expected of you?

No. I was afraid that her parents might make a row and that I might as a consequence lose the studentship I'd just got, and that I would be expelled. Obviously something had to be done, but it was very much on my own conditions.

I never lived a day under the same roof with Susan after we married. It was on my own terms that I married her, and the whole thing quietened down very nicely, largely because of her great good sense and cooperation.

Do you think your son was psychologically damaged by this arrangement?

I don't see why he should have been. He always knew where I was, even if he didn't see me very often, and I've always been on friendly terms with him. He's now well over forty and we go racing together quite often, and we travel abroad together sometimes. He's a very good driver and a good chap to have on a trip, as long as he doesn't drink too much and ask for all the most expensive things on the menu.

About 25 years ago you said: 'The English, by and large, are the last decently behaved people in the world.' Do you still believe that to be true?

I do, despite all the nonsense that goes on. The great danger is so-called political correctness, which could make Nazis of us all in the end. All the informing which goes on, and all the silly judgments which interfere and undermine. I don't think it's too bad in England yet, and on the whole we're still a very decent, tolerant lot.

In your own obituary, which you were invited to write some years ago, you complimented yourself on your loathing for what Orwell called 'smelly little orthodoxies' and what are sometimes called 'modern sensitivities'. What would you include on your list?

The whole bother about race – that's one smelly orthodoxy. I'm perfectly prepared to accept the fact that I need to call anybody of any creed or race equal, but I see no reason why they should be subjects of special consideration. Why on earth should they be? They've got to put up with things like anybody else. The whole business of equality can be solved by decency and commonsense, instead of all this going round making doctrinaire fusses and having special institutions. The Race Relations Board does nothing except make trouble.

Another orthodoxy I have nothing to do with is this matter of equal opportunities for women. If women are as good as men, then let them have the job by all means, but don't make a great sort of fuss about it and say there's got to be a quota. That's a big smelly orthodoxy. And as far as I am concerned, Christianity is another. Belief in Christ is not necessarily smelly, nor is belief in God, but Christianity as it stands is most definitely smelly, from the clap-happies to the most severe Catholics. There are inquisitors in our midst; they may not use heated tongs, but they are inquisitors just the same.

Vicars from HELL

Priests weren't always woolly atheists. **PAUL PICKERING** *remembers a darker and more satanic breed*

Illustration by MARTIN HONEYSETT

I was enjoying the lesson at my local church by the M4 about Shadrach, Meshach and Abednego being thrown into the fiery furnace and then rescued by a mysterious fourth figure, who is obviously an angel, when up jumped the vicar with a Judy Garland smile on

> **During the Cuban missile crisis, the vicar surpassed himself. His message was that nuclear war, although unpleasant, was nothing compared to the wrath of God**

his face. After a quick pout at his nails followed by some of those theatrical little dance steps they seem to teach at ecclesiastical college these days, he demolished, nay, deconstructed the whole wonderful story in a Cambridge sort of way. The 'myth' should not be seen as a piece of magic, oh no. It was, ho hum, political. Just a nice piece of spin-doctoring to make the Jews in Babylon feel good about themselves.

It almost made me yearn for the vicars of my Yorkshire childhood where God was in his heaven, which was 'up there', and anyone falling asleep was prodded with the churchwarden's brass-headed pole; the sort of vicar that is every bit the measure of, and often far worse than, the sin he is combating.

My present priest offers counselling to single-parent families in a manner far different to when my mother lost her first child and became concerned that the baby had not had a proper funeral or been 'churched'. She went to see the vicar in a terrible state and said she had been told the baby would be in purgatory until she herself died. 'Nay,' said the vicar. 'You've got it wrong. Your baby will suffer purgatory until the last judgment.'

Yet that vicar was nothing compared

to a man, now dead, called Halford who took over the parish further up the hill. He had been in the RAF and, having nothing else planned, when the war ended decided to give religion a go. Like all the really top-notch bad vicars his intention was to do good in the little village of Kimberworth

outside Rotherham. At first he did nothing much out of the ordinary. Unlike a minister in Attercliffe he did not pick fights with his congregation to prove whose side God was on. Halford merely wore strange clothes: a black cloak affair of his own design and a three-cornered hat, which was sullenly disapproved of, as was asking parishioners for ten per cent of their income.

But his sermons were so unremittingly horrific that the congregation forgave him. Hard men

who had come through two world wars were apt to stagger out of St Thomas's a little pale. There was no fannying around and shaking hands and the vicar asking what colour you'd painted the kitchen. Everyone went down the semi-perpendicular hill thinking very seriously about Hell and how to avoid it.

The fiery furnace text was always popular in a steel-working area, but during the Cuban missile crisis Halford surpassed himself. He used the tale of Shadrach, Meshach and Abednego to talk about the effects of a heat flash from a nuclear weapon hitting Sheffield and what this might do to Kimberworth, Wentworth and Thorpe Hesley. Several people had to leave.

His message was that nuclear war, although unpleasant, was nothing compared to the wrath of God. In fact Mr Kennedy should not shy away from pressing the button. The 'responsible folk' under their kitchen tables reading the Bible and cheery MOD pamphlets about why not to look at the blast would have the angel sitting by them. 'Unreliable types', which included those in the pub, those who liked Communists, Malcolm Muggeridge, Elvis Presley, and the makers of ungodly radio programmes such as *Hancock's Half Hour*, not to mention 'louts' in milk bars, could expect to run down Kimberworth Hill faster than a fried egg on hot dripping.

Later, drunk on his own popularity, the preacher fell from grace. In the mid-Sixties, as an ill-judged concession to the times probably brought on by one too many conferences on the New Testament, he decided to turn the churchyard into a nature reserve. He banned the old men and their terriers who sat on the churchyard benches. The

men were the backbone of his congregation. The terriers kept down the rats in an area with the highest congregation of rodents in England. Soon the thickets were overrun by a rat population of biblical proportions. There were large, evil-smelling holes in graves, from which we used to try to ignite the gases.

Shunned, Halford took up with a local spinster who owned a spoil heap. Many nights he was to be found in her farmhouse bandaging her phlebitis. He then got himself national publicity by turning away a funeral which had not paid the arbitrary fee he imposed to employ a rat catcher.

The worst priest I have ever known was also a bad man trying to be godly. An ex-South African Air Force officer, he was loosely part of the Verbo Divino Catholic sect in the little town of Hohenau in Paraguay.

One day when I arrived in the town a hymn was in progress in the small church in this mainly German area. Then there was a sharp crack like wood splitting. Next a man was being carried from the church swearing. Father Wolfgang filled the doorway with his hands clasped in front of him and an expression of tender regret on his face in the manner of priests all over

the world. Except Wolfgang's hands contained a smoking Colt 45.

I learned later that he had shot the man – 'only in the leg' – for talking in church. Naturally Wolfgang, who did not have a symbolic bone in his body, believed Christ paid for all our sins on the cross which, like the fiery furnace, was as real as his warm gun. Very soon Wolfgang himself expected to be searching for the exit and the angel. Is this more reassuring than my present C of E atheist? Well, as my grandad used to say, 'If that's the sort of help God employs then there's hope for the rest of us.'

AD LIB – *ad infinitum*

On the opening night of Oblomov, **SPIKE MILLIGAN** *walked on stage, forgot all his lines, and turned a serious drama into an unprecedented comic triumph.* **IAN FLINTOFF** *was in the cast*

The curtain came down for the interval, and Spike Milligan walked off stage while the standing-room-only house clapped, laughed and roared. He got into his Mini – parked near the stage door – drove home to Finchley and did not return. As a very young actor, I spent a couple of years in a West End play of which he was the star.

Oblomov had been adapted by the Italian writer Riccardo Aragno from the nineteenth-century Russian novel by Goncharov. Spike's firm had bought the script to launch him as a straight and sensitive actor, playing the part of a Russian aristocrat who couldn't be bothered to get out of bed. Joan Greenwood took the female lead, and other major parts were played by Bill Owen and Valentine Dyall. It was a major production for a young impresario, Michael White. The director was Frank Dunlop, who went on to do magnificent work at the Edinburgh Festival.

On the morning of the read-through, Frank spoke of the delicate and sensitive Chekhovian nature of the piece and, for the six or seven weeks of rehearsal, that was the kind of production we were all aiming for.

We opened at the Lyric Hammersmith. On the first night Spike, overwhelmed by stage fright, forgot every line. The rest of us were thrown, but he kept going, making up the missing lines as he went along. Spotting the *Evening Standard*'s critic, Milton Shulman, in the audience, and in gratitude for previous rave notices, he declared: 'Thank God, Milton Shulman's in!'

The notices were generally unkind, but since the show was booked for several weeks, Michael White and Frank Dunlop proposed to save it by allowing Spike complete *carte blanche* on stage. Spike ad-libbed his way through every performance. *Oblomov*, changed beyond recognition, ran for five weeks and broke all the Lyric's box-office records, before being transferred to the West End as *Son of Oblomov*. It could still be running to this day had the exhausting job that Spike took upon himself not made this humanly impossible. No two performances were the same. Audiences – including the Prince of Wales – could return time and again and see a different show. As a result, there was never a feeling of audiences falling off. *Son of Oblomov* epitomised Spike at his best: inventive, unpredictable and indefatigable.

My first scene was alone with him on stage. I'd dutifully learned my lines in response to fixed cues, but, since Spike couldn't be bothered with anything like cues, you got what you were given – which was invariably followed by drowning laughter from the audience. If you were tempted to come in a milli-second too soon and kill the laugh, he'd gently mumble from the side of his mouth: 'Wait for it, wait for it.'

Once I entered stage right to find that Spike was sitting in the stalls, in his nightgown costume, calling up to me, 'Come on then, Ian, give us a

Spike Milligan with co-star Marjie Lawrence in *Son of Oblomov*

show!' Another time I did the routine business – came on, sat down, extended my hand without looking to shake his as I'd done 100 times – and his hand came off in mine.

The Queen and family came on her birthday, with Peter Sellers and Britt Ekland. Spike set up a double-act routine with Sellers across the heads in the front stalls – 'Why does the Duke of Edinburgh wear red, white and blue braces?' 'I don't know. Why does the Duke of Edinburgh wear red, white and blue braces?' 'To keep his trousers up!' The show overran by 45 minutes.

Spike was kind and generous to younger members of the cast, myself included. My first impression of him was of a painfully shy, quiet, gentle, almost diffident man – though an old mate of his, the Australian Bill Kerr who was later co-opted into the cast, once said to me, 'We have to put up with all the shit, mate, because it pays the rent'.

I suspect that Spike was then searching for a full expression of another side of himself: the man who personally repainted the children's Elfin Oak in Kensington Gardens, at his own expense and with an anonymous plaque claiming that the work was 'done by the fairies'; who sat down on pavements in protest against the threats of extinction to wildlife; who never forgot his friends when they needed work and he could help.

Though all this happened a long time ago, I've forgotten none of it – and I never will. Next time I'm on stage Spike's 'Wait for it, wait for it' will whisper to me still.

'No credit cards? You some kind of nut?'

THE DEATH FILE

*The original University Challenge presenter and author **BAMBER GASCOIGNE** contemplates that final question on which there is no conferring*

MY IDEAL WAY TO GO...

A few months ago my computer gave me a glimpse of an ideal way to go. I had more than three years' work in a database called Ency\Ency. But the screen declared: 'Ency\ Ency does not exist.' Vanished. Snuffed out. Just like that. And painlessly, it seemed, from the point of view of the database – though not from mine. The human equivalent has to be a heart attack. I am told you can be pruning your roses and dead before you hit the ground. My equivalent of roses is hunched over the computer, so that must be the place as well as the method.

MY LIFE EXPECTANCY...

Ranges from five minutes to 35 years.

MY LAST WORDS...

Ideal way to go precludes.

MY METHOD OF DISPOSAL...

I like the idea of books in a necrobibliotech. People's remains would be in book-shaped containers on shelves, with their names on the spine and a decent catalogue for browsers and researchers to find their way around.

MY FUNERAL ARRANGEMENTS...

The Humanist Association provides sympathetic 'ministers' who will conduct a dignified farewell based on some of the greatest passages in English literature.

MY SPECIAL EFFECTS...

Fewer than in life. No starters for ten.

MEMORIAL SERVICE...

An event that all my friends go away from feeling much better than when they came. Only one condition: they must all wish I'd been there (frequently and aloud).

THE OTHER SIDE?...

I imagine D-Day +1 as being like sleep, but without the pleasure of waking up and discovering there is time to go to sleep again.

MY THOUGHTS ON LIFE AND DEATH...

I believe life to be meaningless but utterly fascinating. Compared to the improbability of having won the original race, as the first spermatozoon to reach the egg of the month, the certainty of death is trivial.

Myth

A short story by **RUTH RENDELL**

Illustrations by **PETER BAILEY**

The monk and the interpreter moved on; through the library, through the refectory, out into the cloisters. The party followed. Flaking frescoes and faded murals were pointed out, their provenance explained. The hot sun was white and trembling on the stone flags, the shadows black. Thankfully, the party surged into the shop.

There were no tea towels or tablecloths or aprons or even calendars of the map of the Garden of Eden, but there were postcards and lifesize facsimiles. Framed or unframed.

'You don't really want one, do you?' Rosemary said.

'Yes, of course I do.' David had taken to barking at her lately, especially if, as now, she seemed even mildly to oppose his wishes. 'I think it's very beautiful, a marvellous piece of history.'

'As you wish.'

He bought a framed map and then, on second thoughts, an unframed map as well and four postcards. Back at the hotel he got her to pack the framed map, parcelled in bubble-wrap and their clothes, into their carry-on bag. The unframed map he spread out on the desk top, weighting down its corners with the ashtray, two glasses and the stand that held the room service menu. He sat down with his elbows on the desk and studied the map. After dinner, instead of going to the bar, he went back to their room and she found him there later, crouched over the desk. From somewhere or other he had procured a magnifying glass.

She was pleased. He had found something to take him out of himself. These were probably early days to think of a hobby developing from it, that he might begin collecting old maps, antiquarian books, something like that. But surely this was how such things began.

She vaguely remembered hearing that an uncle of hers had started collecting stamps because a friend sent him a letter from Outer Mongolia. If only David would find an interest!

Since the loss of his job, he had been a changed man, sullen, bad-tempered, sometimes savage in his manner towards her. And he had been very unhappy. The large sum of money he received in compensation, the golden handshake, had done nothing to mitigate his misery. He still spoke daily of the Chief Executive, a young woman, walking into his office, telling him to clear his desk and go.

> ## She looked at the library books and the books he had bought. Every one of them was concerned with the Garden of Eden

'I'll never forget it,' he said. 'Her face, that red mouth like a slice of raw beef, and that tight bright blue suit showing her fat knees. And her voice, not a word of excuse or apology, not a hint of shame.'

Rosemary saw to her horror that he had tears in his eyes. She thought it would help when the cheque that came was twice what he expected. She thought he might put those humiliating events behind him once she had found the beautiful house in Wiltshire and driven him there and shown him. But apathy had succeeded rage, and then rage came back alternating with periods of deep depression. He sat about all day or he paced. In the evenings he watched television indiscriminately. His doctor suggested this holiday, two weeks in the Aegean before the move.

'I don't care,' he said. 'If you like. It's all one to me. I'll never get her voice out of my head, not a word of apology, no shame.'

He rolled up the map of the Garden of Eden and she packed it in his suitcase. What became of the postcards she didn't know until she saw him studying one of them on the plane.

They moved house two weeks after their return. It was only his second visit to the house, only the second time he had walked through these spacious rooms and down the steps from the terrace onto the lawn to look across at the seven acres which were now his. Wasn't this better than living in a north London terrace, taking the Northern Line daily to a Docklands office? She wasn't so tactless as to ask him directly. It put heart into her to see him explore the place, pronounce later that evening that it wasn't so bad, that it was a relief to breathe fresh air.

She busied herself getting the place straight, unpacking the boxes, deciding where this piece of furniture and that should go. Two men arrived to hang the new curtains. Another brought the chandelier, holland-wrapped, tied up with string. He hung it in the drawing-room and he hung the pictures. David hung up his framed map of the Garden of Eden in the room that was going to be his study. Then he asked the man to hang a much bigger picture he had and which he wanted in the dining-room. Rosemary saw, to her surprise, that it was the map again, but blown up to three times its size (and therefore rather vague and blurred) in an ornate gilt frame.

'I had it done,' David said. 'Last week. I found a place where they photocopy things to any size you want.'

She was overjoyed. If she felt a

talist work, a modern novel called *Rib Into Woman*, Milton's *Paradise Lost* and several others. Well, she had hoped he would take up a hobby, that he would study something or collect something, and what it appeared he was studying was evidently – paradise.

Presumably, he would tell her about it sooner or later. He would say what the purpose of it was, what he meant to do with it, what he expected to accomplish. They had enough to live on comfortably, he had no need of an earned income, but perhaps he intended to write a book for his own pleasure. She watched him. She didn't ask. Her own life was less busy than it had been in London and it took concentration to find enough to do. She must become involved with village life, she thought, find charity work, develop her own interests. He didn't seem to want her to help in the garden. Meanwhile, she cooked more than she ever had, baked their bread, made jam from the soft fruit. She admitted to herself that she was lonely.

But when, at last, he did tell her, it came as a shock. She said, 'I don't understand. I don't know what you mean.'

'Just what I say.' He had stopped barking at her. He habitually spoke gently now, even dreamily. 'It's here. The Garden is here. This is where it is. It's taken me a few weeks to be sure, that's why I've said nothing till now. But now I am absolutely certain. The Garden of Eden is there, outside our windows.'

'David,' she said, 'the Garden of Eden doesn't exist. It never did exist. It is a myth. You know that as well as I do.'

He looked at her with narrowed eyes, as if he suspected her mental equilibrium.

'Why do you say that?'

'Believing in it as a real place is like saying Adam and Eve really existed.'

'Why not?' he said.

'David, I'm not hearing this. You can't be saying this. Listen, people used to believe in it. Then Darwin came along and his theory of evolution, you know that. You know that God, if there is a God, didn't make a man out of whatever it is...'

'Dust.'

'Well, dust, all right. He didn't take out one of his ribs and make a woman. I mean, it's laughable. Only crazy sects believe that stuff.' She stopped,

---

tremor of unease it was a tiny thing, brought about surely by her heightened nervousness and sensitivity to his moods. If she was ever so slightly disturbed by the spectacle of a man of fifty engrossed in a cheap copy of a map of some mythical place... But no, it was wonderful to see him returning to his old self, to interest and occupation. He even arranged the furniture in his study, put his books out on the shelves. By nine next morning he was out in the garden, and later in the day off in the car to a nursery where there was a chance of finding some particular shrub he wanted.

After they had been in the new place a week she realised he hadn't once mentioned the Chief Executive or her mouth or her blue suit or her voice. So this, apparently, was the solution. Not the holiday or the doctor's drugs or even kindness but the move to somewhere new and different. His days, which had been empty, gradually became busy and filled. He followed a pattern, gardening in the morning and in the afternoon

going out in the car and returning with books. Some came from a library, some he bought. She paid them very little attention. It was enough to know that he was reading again after not opening a book of any kind for months. Then one day he asked her if they had a Bible in the house.

She was astonished. Neither of them had religious leanings. 'Your old school Bible is somewhere. Shall I look for it?'

'I will,' he said, and then, 'I want to look something up.'

He found the Bible and was soon immersed in it. Perhaps he was about to undergo some sort of conversion. This house was his road to Damascus. Disquiet returned in a small niggling way and when he was outside mowing the lawn next day she looked at the library books and the books he had bought. Every one of them was concerned in some respect or other with the Garden of Eden. There was a scholarly examination of the book of Genesis, an American Fundamen-

thought. 'You're joking, aren't you, you're having me on?'

In a rapt, dreamy tone, as if she hadn't spoken, he said, 'It's always been believed that the site of the Garden was somewhere in the Middle East because Genesis mentions the River Euphrates and Ethiopia and Assyria. But, seriously, how could a garden be in Syria and Ethiopia and Iraq all at the same time? The truth is that it was far away, in a place they knew nothing of, a distant place beyond the confines of the known world...'

'Wiltshire,' she said.

'Please don't mock,' he said. 'Cynicism doesn't suit you. Come outside and I'll show you.'

He took the Bible with him and one of the postcards. The area of their land he led her to comprised the old orchard, a lawn and the water garden, through which two spring-fed streams flowed. She saw that the lawn had been mown and the banks of the streams tidied up. It was very pretty, a lush mature garden in which unusual plants grew and where fruit trees against the old wall bore ripening plums and pears.

'There, you see,' he said, referring to his Bible, 'is the river called Pison, that is it which compasseth the whole land of Havilah, where there is gold.' His eyes flashed. There was sweat on his upper lip. 'And the name of the second river is Gihon, and the third Hiddekel and the fourth river is Euphrates.'

She could only see two, not much more than trickles, flowing over English stones among English water butter-cups. He turned and beckoned to her in his old peremptory way but his voice was still measured and gentle. His voice was as if he was explaining something obvious to a slow-witted child.

'There,' he said, 'the Tree of Life. Sometimes we call it the tree of the knowledge of good and evil.'

He pointed to it and led her up under its branches, a big old apple tree, laden with small green apples. When first she saw the house she remembered it had been in blossom.

> **'There,' he said, 'the Tree of Life. Sometimes we call it the tree of the knowledge of good and evil'**

'Mustn't eat those, eh?'

His smile and his short bark of laughter frightened her. She felt entirely at a loss. This was the man she had been married to for twenty years, the practical clever businessman. How had he known those words, how had he known where to look for this – this web of nonsense? She put out her hand and touched the tree. She hung on to it, leaned against it, for she was afraid she might faint.

'I wondered when I first discovered it,' he said, 'if we were being given a second chance.'

She didn't know what he meant. She closed her eyes, bowed her head.

When she felt she could breathe again and that strength was returning, she looked for him but he was gone. She made her way back to the house. Later, after he had gone to bed, she sat downstairs, wondering what to do. It couldn't be right for him to be left to go on like this. But in the morning when she woke and he woke, when they encountered each other on adjoining pillows, then across the breakfast table, he seemed his normal self. He talked about taking on a gardener, the place was too much for him alone. Would she like the dining-room redecorated? She had said she disliked the wallpaper. And perhaps it was time to invite the neighbours in – if you could call people living half a mile away neighbours – have a small drinks party, acquaint themselves with the village.

She summoned up all the courage she had. 'That was a game you were playing last evening, wasn't it? You weren't serious?'

He laughed. 'You evidently didn't think I was.' It was hardly an answer. 'I dreamt of that bitch,' he said. 'She came in wearing that ghastly blue suit that showed her fat knees and told me to clear my desk. She was eating an apple – did I tell you that?'

'In your dream, do you mean?'

He was instantly angry. 'No, I don't mean that. In reality is what I mean. She came into my office with an apple in her hand, she was eating an apple. I told you.'

She shook her head. He had never told her that, she would have remembered. Next day the new gardener started. She was afraid David would say something to him about the Garden of Eden. When neighbours came in for drinks a week later she was afraid David would say something to them. He didn't. It seemed that conversation on this subject was reserved to her alone. With other people he was genial, bland, civilised. In the evenings, alone with her, he spent his time compiling a list of the plants indigenous to Eden, balm and pomegranate, coriander and hyssop. He took her into the fruit garden and showed her the fig tree that grew up against the wall, pointing out its hand-shaped leathery leaves and saying that they could stitch the leaves together and make themselves aprons.

She looked that up in Genesis and found the reference. Then she went to seek advice.

The doctor didn't take her seriously. Or he didn't take David's obsession seriously. He said he would review the tranquillisers he was already prescribing for David and this he did – with startling effect. David's enthusiasm seemed to wane, he became quiet and preoccupied, busied himself in other areas of the grounds, returned to his old interest of reading biographies. He joined the golf club. He no longer spoke of the Chief Executive and her blue suit and her apple. The only thing to disquiet Rosemary was the snake.

'I've just seen an adder,' he told her when he came in for his lunch. 'Curled up under the fig tree.'

She said nothing, just looked at him.

'It might have been a grass snake, I'm not sure, but it was certainly a snake.'

'Is it still there?'

There came a flash of the bad temper she hadn't seen for weeks. 'How do I know if it's still there? Come and see.'

Not a snake, but a shed snake skin. Nothing could have made Rosemary happier. She was so certain the snake was part of his delusion, but he had seen a real snake, or a real snake's skin. He was well again, it was over, whatever it had been.

The summer had been long and hot and the fruit crop was spectacular. First the raspberries and gooseberries, then peaches and plums. Rosemary made jam and jelly, she even bottled fruit the way her mother used to. None of it must be wasted. David picked the pears before they were ripe, wrapped each one individually in tissue paper and stored them in boxes.

The days were long and golden, the evenings mild and the air scented with ripe fruit. David often walked round the grounds at dusk but that was the merest coincidence, it had nothing to do with the Lord God walking in the garden at the cool of the day.

The big tree was a Cox, David thought, a Cox's Orange Pippin, considered by many even today to be the finest English apple. It was laden with fruit. They used an apple picker with a ten-foot handle but they had to put a ladder up into the highest branches. Rosemary went up it because she was the lighter of them and the more agile. He held the ladder and she picked.

> **Fed by the streams he had called Pison and Gihon, Hiddekel and Euphrates, it was an ideal home for her Koi carp**

If her fears hadn't been allayed, if she hadn't put the whole business of the map and the Garden of Eden behind her – and, come to that, the Chief Executive in her bright blue suit – she might have been more cautious. She might have been wary. She had forgotten that cryptic remark of his when he said that they – meaning mankind? – might have been given a second chance. She had come to see his delusion as the temporary madness of a man humiliated and driven beyond endurance. So she climbed down the

ladder with her basket of shiny red and gold fruit and taking one in her hand, a flawless ripe apple, held it out to him and said, 'Look at that, isn't that absolutely perfect? Try it, have a bite.'

His face grew dark red and swollen. He shouted, 'You won't do it a second time, woman, you won't bring evil into the world a second time!'

He lashed out at her with the apple picker, struck her on the side of the head, on the shoulder, again on her head. She fell to the ground and the apples spilled out and rolled everywhere. Her screams fetched the gardener who got there just in time, pulled David off, wrested the bloodstained apple picker out of his hands.

Rosemary was in hospital for a long time but not so long as David. When she was better she went to see him. He was in the day room, quiet and subdued, watching a game show on television. When he saw her he picked up the first weapon that came to hand, a table lamp, brandished it and flung himself upon her, cursing her and crying that he would multiply her sorrow. They advised her not to go back and she never did.

She stayed in the house on her own, she liked it. After all, she had chosen it in the first place. But she took the maps of the Garden of Eden out of their frames and gave the frames to the village jumble sale. In the spring she had the apple tree cut down and made a big fishpond where it had stood. Fed by the streams he had called Pison and Gihon, Hiddekel and Euphrates, it was an ideal home for her Koi carp which became the envy of the county.

THE SPY WHO SAVED THE WEST

DOUGLAS STUART *reveals how double agent* **KIM PHILBY** *tipped off Stalin and changed the course of the Second World War…*

Kim Philby's passport photograph, taken by Jane Bown

I knew Kim Philby, but then who of my generation of foreign correspondents didn't? His family nickname came from Kipling's novel whose eponymous hero was 'little friend of all the world'. Kim collected friends as he collected wives. He needed to be liked and loved. With reservations, my wife and I did like him. In the late Fifties, Kim was appointed Middle East correspondent of the *Economist* and the *Observer*, and throughout the Beirut summer of 1958 we formed a working coalition to report the Lebanese civil war. About spying, he was mute. Everyone accepted that he

was still at it – for the British, of course. But he talked to us 'frankly' about his involvement in the defection to Moscow of Burgess and Maclean, naturally insisting on his 'innocence'. It wasn't until he himself fled to Moscow in 1963 that Kim spoke of his espionage coup in the winter of 1941 which triggered the slow but sure defeat of Hitler's armies.

The story begins in May 1941, when Richard Sorge, Tokyo correspondent of the *Frankfurter Zeitung* and Soviet spy, warned Moscow that a German attack on the Soviet Union was imminent. Stalin refused to believe him. He also dismissed the

British government's warnings to the same effect. Six months later, 78 German divisions halted on the outskirts of Moscow, exhausted, frozen and short of ammunition, food and petrol; but morale was high. Everyone confidently believed that they had crushed Soviet resistance. And then on 5th December the Soviet High Command launched a counter-attack across the snow and ice with new guns, new tanks and a million fit new men.

The Germans retreated up to a hundred miles. Their losses were enormous: up to 750,000 casualties and a quarter of all their tanks and artillery. Panzer General Heinz Guderian wrote in his diary: 'We have suffered a serious defeat.' It was more than that. It was the turning-point of the conflict. As the Germans came to terms with their first defeat, the Japanese bombed Pearl Harbor and Hitler declared war on the United States.

Strategically the Soviet victory outside Moscow was made possible by the intelligence supplied by two spies: Sorge in Moscow and Philby in London. In October, Sorge reported that the Japanese proposed to strike south and therefore posed no further threat to the Soviet eastern front. Once again Stalin refused to believe him. In November, however, as German troops advanced swiftly towards Moscow, Philby sent the NKVD the text of an intercepted telegram. It was from the German ambassador in Tokyo to Berlin and it gave the same information about Japanese intentions as Sorge had done. With this confirmation Stalin ordered all troops in the Far East, Siberia and Central Asia to the defence of Moscow. More than twenty years later Philby told the Soviet journalist, Genrikh Borovnik, that the Tokyo–Berlin telegram was the most valuable information he ever sent to Moscow.

These are the facts: or are they?

Self-portrait by Raymond Briggs, 1999

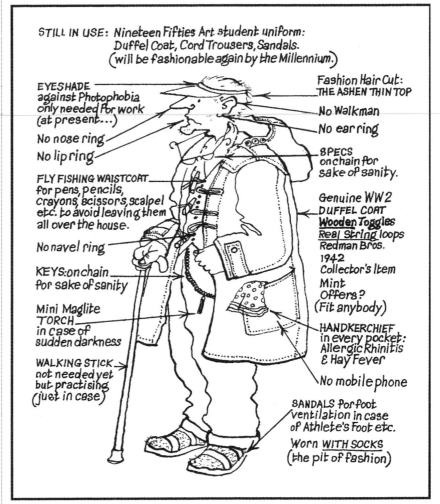

The world of espionage, in the words of James Angleton of the CIA, is a 'wilderness of mirrors'. From personal knowledge I can testify to Kim Philby's ability to tell almost the truth. For example, in his interview with Borovnik he says: 'My report was independently confirmed by Sorge from Japan.' Untrue: Sorge reported a month before Philby.

Then there's the question of how Philby got hold of the intercept. The telegram was part of Ultra, the top secret information produced by the code-breakers of Bletchley. Ultra distribution was carefully controlled and carefully guarded. In November 1941 Philby was stationed in St Albans,

> **I can testify to Kim Philby's ability to tell almost the truth**

dealing with counter-espionage in Spain, Portugal and their islands in the Atlantic. It seems highly improbable that he was given access to Ultra and even more unlikely that he could steal, copy and return Ultra documents. Could he have been given the intercept to pass on to Moscow? His bosses in SIS realised that anything from official British sources would be rejected by Stalin. It could be argued, therefore, why not try a Soviet source? And if they turned to Philby, doesn't this suggest that they knew all along that he was working for the NKVD?

In Moscow, the Philby puzzle was approached from another angle. The NKVD analyst Yelena Modrzhinskaya spent two years checking all Philby's reports, coming to the conclusion that they were too good to be true and that he was a British Intelligence plant. Eventually Philby was cleared. But the trouble with double agents is that nobody really trusts them. After Philby's flight to Moscow, even Donald Maclean accused his fellow Cambridge spy of continuing to work for the British. The KGB kept him under careful watch until his death a quarter of a century after his defection. They used him as a propaganda vehicle against the West. They gave him money, medals and special treatment, but they never thanked him for helping to win the Second World War.

Notes from the sofa

by RAYMOND BRIGGS

SEVENTY YEARS AGO I was evacuated to two spinster 'aunties' in Dorset. As a five-year-old I looked upon them as very old ladies, but years later I realised they can only have been in their forties. They were two of the thousands of women condemned to spinsterhood by the Great War. For a child at that time the world seemed to be full of aunties.

They lived in a small stone cottage of only three rooms, with massive walls, tiny windows and a curving stone staircase.

The week I arrived the aunties were rejoicing that, at long last, the one and only cold tap had been moved inside the cottage. This, together with the luxury of a sink and a state-of-the-art plug hole.

Cooking was done on a gas stove fed by a cylinder that also provided two feeble gas mantles. Upstairs in the one bedroom, there was no lighting. The wireless was powered by a massive glass battery and, because of the expense, was switched on only once a

day for the nine o'clock news.

The simplicity of life then seems almost unbelievable today. Just listing the things that were not there: no television, LPs, CDs or cassettes. No music at all. No central heating, fridge, freezer, washing-machine, dishwasher or vacuum cleaner. No oil or electricity. No telephone.

Also, there was no bathroom, shower or flush lavatory. The only heating was the coal fire in the living room, with a blackened kettle always sitting on it.

The lavatory was an Elsan in a tin shed under the apple tree. A farm worker came and emptied it once in a while. No one was allowed to urinate in it or it would have filled up in a day or two. I was told to pee in the hedge and the very ladylike aunties peed in a bucket in the kitchen.

Primitive it may have been, but at least there was no computer, email or internet. Also, there were no holidays, no shop and no car. One bus a week.

Paradise Lost.

BERKMANN   WHEEN   HISLOP   BOOKER

PRIVATE EYE   0

ITV/REX FEATURES

Universally challenged?

The young have a lot to learn, admits **JEREMY PAXMAN**. *But don't feel so smug – how many of you oldies can identify Schrödinger or explain Planck's Constant?*

I suspect I've been asked to write this piece because the Editor thinks it will enable *Oldie* readers to feel smug. As a dedicated viewer of *University Challenge*, he claims frequently to be astonished by the fact that so many of the contestants don't know things which he had thought were common knowledge, like who had the fourth highest batting average in the 1949 England cricket tour of South Africa.

As the students look blank, the Editor sits at home, like all *Oldie* readers, thwacking the arm of his Parker Knoll Recliner, screaming at the television, 'It's Crapp, Crapp, Crapp, you fools.' We cannot all aspire to the Editor's ability to recognise the euphonious Gloucestershire left-hander, J F Crapp. But I suspect he is accurate in his vision of people across the nation hurling their cups of Ovaltine at the television screen with cries of 'What on earth do they teach young people nowadays?'

I share the irritation about some of the questions one is expected to ask. Why an ability to recall the canon of Fat Boy Slim is thought by the producers to be evidence of intellectual achievement is a mystery. It probably has something

to do with the fact that the programme was commissioned by the BBC's 'Youth' department. Whoever's responsible, it's hardly the students' fault that they can answer the questions.

I confess that sometimes I, too, am astonished by what they don't know. The other week we had a music round entirely made up of three of the best-known hymns in Christendom. No one was able to identify the starter question, and when the bonus questions were eventually allocated, they all fell to Keble College, Oxford. This being an institution built in memory of the founder of the Oxford Movement, you might have expected the Keble students to make a clean sweep. Instead of which, the best and the brightest the college could produce sat dumbly as one hymn after another echoed around the studio. They might as well have been a collection of Aztec prayer chants.

What do we conclude from these astonishing lapses? Are all students nowadays irredeemably ignorant? I'm sorry to disappoint. But it has been a sad fact of the British educational system for decades that in order to qualify for university you need only to be able to appear plausible to a bunch of lecturers who know little or nothing outside

their specialised field. The idea of the general education which produced the well-rounded mind was smothered when A-levels were invented. We should have to admit, too, that, as the number of universities has expanded, the level of intellectual achievement has gone down. How could it be otherwise, when the proportion of the school age population going on to tertiary education has risen almost tenfold?

> **What do we conclude from their astonishing lapses? Are all students nowadays irredeemably ignorant?**

Although all the student teams on *University Challenge* have had to qualify by passing an entry exam, the chasm between the highest-scoring qualifiers and the lowest is vast. In the early stages of the competition, there are bound to be embarrassments. There is nothing worse than sitting there asking question after question as one team fails to provide a single correct answer. But there does come a point – when the scores are 200 against minus

The *Private Eye* team on *University Challenge – The Professionals*, 2005. From left: Marcus Berkmann, Francis Wheen, Ian Hislop and Christopher Booker

ten – when the thing acquires the awful fascination of a car crash.

Yet even among the better teams there can be astonishing lacunae. How, do you think, can they not know the date of the Battle of Crécy, or Tennyson's first name?

But all knowledge exists in a cultural context. Even Pythagoras, Einstein, Mozart or Goethe must, very occasionally, have exclaimed, 'Well, I never knew that!' And since no one can be expected to know everything, the question is merely which things some of them do know.

Clearly, times have changed. The average contestant seems to know a lot less about classical mythology than you might have expected forty years ago. But they know a great deal more about science. They may have no idea who Sisyphus was, but they can probably identify Schrödinger.

Before you hurl your mug at the television, remember two things. Firstly, that (with one or two exceptions – that 'perpetual student' really does exist and is even now signing up for a tenth degree somewhere or other) they are all a lot younger than you. It's all very well attacking them for not knowing something you fondly imagine you might have known at the age of twenty. But how many armchair critics, with the luxury of another twenty, thirty or forty years, can explain Planck's Constant? They ought to be able to do so. Knowledge, as much as wisdom, accumulates over the years.

And secondly, it's a damn sight easier watching at home shouting out the answers than it is sitting in a tense television studio knowing that if you get it wrong half the Student Union will refuse to share their pork scratchings with you. One team, from another Oxford college, fielded a Catholic priest who, while he seemed to know almost everything about Josephine Baker, was unable to identify the Magnificat. Nerves can do that to you.

No, I think I am going to disappoint *The Oldie*'s distinguished Editor. Armchair criticism of the 'Bah, students nowadays know nothing' variety is as valid as a capon's comments on why the cockerel failed to get the hens laying.

Thoughts on death

Even at my age, says **PHILIP CALLOW**, *I persist in thinking that death is something that happens to other people*

IF I TELL MYSELF, as I sometimes do, that thoughts of death have occupied my mind with some regularity over the past years, I know I am only stating the obvious. In 1989 my wife suffered an awful blow, losing her daughter to meningitis in her 21st year. Since then we have tended her grave more or less fortnightly.

There is something monstrous about a young person cut down on the very threshold of life. Kneeling at the graveside cutting grass, planting snowdrop bulbs, I ask myself how this can be. Why should I be spared, my days numbered, and this vibrant girl be in her grave?

Thirty years ago, in the throes of a complete breakdown, I contemplated ending it all as the only way out. But even the worthless life that mine then seemed to be was stronger than death. The inexorable law of life is that we must live, even when we are utterly without hope. 'One day,' my doctor told me, 'you'll look at the world with new eyes.' And so it turned out to be. The force which drives us as it drives the sun and the stars is almost impossible to withstand.

So, of course, is death, and that is the paradox. Death approaches like a force embedded deep in the earth. In fact, life and death seem to be speaking the same language, so dependent are they on each other. Winter gives birth to spring: a seed falls to the ground and from its little death a flame of growth spurts up.

I subscribe to no conventional religion, I have no belief in a personal God, yet the grand majesty of old hymns can inspire me. If I find it hard to believe in oblivion waiting for us at the end of existence, it is because there are no full stops in nature. Somehow we are part of something endlessly flowing. And for me the laughable thing is this: even now, in spite of my age and the evidence of death all around me, I can't imagine being dead.

Death is something that happens to other people. Of course if I had a chronic illness it would be different. When we are young we feel immortal, and that is perfectly natural, but to feel it at my age is absurd. Yet I do.

I cannot imagine an afterlife, but nor can I deny its possibility in some form we cannot possibly grasp, mired as we are in our senses and unable to comprehend anything beyond the scope of the life we know. What if my spirit shoots off into space after death and joins billions of others? There is room for us all out there. What if it swoops

> *I should like to return as a ghost in order to reward my wife in some way for her forbearance*

into a newborn baby at the moment of birth, as more than one religion believes? The vitality which determines our existence cannot be measured or explained by science, coming as it does from a Fourth Dimension, which a Christian would call the Holy Ghost. If my spirit wanders forth to seek another incarnation after my body has expired, why not? But to my wife this is anathema. Once is enough! she cries.

A writer's devious nature is not easy to live with and, after my death, I should like to return as a ghost in order to reward my wife in some way for her forbearance, if the lords of death will allow me. I hope when my time comes I will summon up some courage. I am comforted by the thought of Walt Whitman, lying paralysed for years, who could even joke on good days about his slipping hold on life, telling his young Boswell, 'As Miss Nipper says in *Dombey and Son*, I don't know whether I am temporary or a permanency: I don't know whether I am to stay or move on.'

RESTAURANT

BAR

Espresso BONKERS

... you must be, says **JOAN WYNDHAM**, *to want to run a restaurant*

Illustrations by Larry

To anyone mad enough to think of opening a restaurant, my advice would be a definite 'Don't!' However, if the urge is too strong to resist, here are a few tips. It's true that I know little of the super-smart places that I can't afford, or the super-trendy ones where I can't get in. What I have done is to run (and cook in) three totally loony and eccentric restaurants – La Roma in Oxford, Etcetera in the Portobello Road and The Gasworks in Fulham – where I learnt a lot, most of it unpleasant.

Location, of course, is all-important, so copy the Chinese and call in a top-class feng shui expert. Let's say you've picked something in the lower reaches of the Fulham Road. You are bang opposite the Brompton Cemetery, the undertakers and the Catholic Church, and next door to the Chinese Hospital. A feng shui disaster! You wouldn't stand a chance. But, you protest, it's near Stamford Bridge! How about all those hungry Chelsea fans queuing up for my goodies after a match? Sorry, no way! If they've won, they'll go streaming down to the Chelsea Tup (aka The Sheepshaggers Arms) to celebrate by getting royally pissed, and if beaten, slink home despondently to raid the fridge.

> **The students roosted like chickens among the potato sacks, their noses stuck into Nietzsche**

So you decide to take a look at the other end of the road, mysteriously known as 'the Beach' and dedicated to the cult of 'yoof', as it used to be called. Unfortunately the young are not too interested in gourmet food and seem quite happy with an espresso and a fag, provided the music is loud enough. So what you can do is open a huge bar in the basement with even louder music and elastic closing hours. Soon it will be packed with regulars having a nightly rave-up – all the thrill of a club without having to pay membership, and you can sit happily upstairs in your empty restaurant, listening to the manic tinkling of the cash register below.

There are, of course, a few old-fashioned romantics, with visions of creating a cosy but profitable little haven – candlelight and Vivaldi, tables full of friends to chat to and rave reviews from Fay Maschler. As they probably don't realise what a back-breaking grind it's going to be, I'd like to give them some advice. First, premises: you've been told about rising damp and dry rot, but how about vermin? Before signing, spend a night in the kitchen, and if the darkness lights up with little red eyes and you hear the rustle of cockroaches, think again. Then look carefully into plumbing, as crossed connections can lead to the most unsavoury consequences. As, for example, the lady living underneath a Chinese restaurant whose bathroom overflow got confused with the kitchen sink, and who found herself relaxing in a bubble bath full of bean sprouts and bamboo shoots.

Make the kitchen as large as possible. I have dreadful memories of the four-foot-square sweat-box I once cooked in, where you could boil, bake, fry and grill while standing on one spot, waving your arms about like Toscanini conducting the 1812. Two fridges – one for fish – are always a good idea, so that the chef won't have to waste valuable time picking frozen shrimps out of the lemon syllabub.

Talking of chefs, beware of prima-donnas who think of themselves as some kind of minor royalty, terrorising the staff and running up ruinous bills for black truffles and foie gras. Try to keep the food as simple as possible. A customer who rashly orders char-grilled frogs' legs couched on a souflette of pak choi and papaya with a sesame and lemon-grass dressing may feel his taste-buds briefly tingling, but after waiting for at least 45 minutes – all small-talk with his date exhausted – he'll feel ready to kill for a short-order plateful of bangers and mash.

As regards staff, there are no hard-and-fast rules, but certain classes of person are best avoided, such as pregnant ladies, young men with mauve hair and diamanté dog-collars, or sullen-eyed blondes escorted by boyfriends in black leather and bicycle chains.

To keep the kitchen staff sober, avoid too many dishes like boeuf bourgignon and coq au vin, which give them unlimited access to the cooking plonk. Keep flambéed creations to a minimum, or one

day you may see your chef crawling on all fours between the stove and the serving hatch, a platter of flaming bananas balanced on his head.

Train your waiters to be nice to everyone, except for rude, noisy drunks, and even smile at obvious no-nos, such as ageing hippies who bring their own chopsticks and carry their money in a matchbox. They should be particularly nice to pretty young girls on their own, anyone looking like a celeb or a food critic, men in Armani suits with designer stubble, old friends, lavish tippers and women in power suits and pashminas who like to smoke cigars and order their own wine. But one thing you must forbid them to do

" Even smile at obvious no-nos, such as the ageing hippies who carry their money in a matchbox "

at all costs is to interrupt interesting conversations with that meaningless remark, 'Everything all right?'

Another of my pet hates is red-hot plates served straight from the microwave. I have always believed that food tastes better the cooler it gets – probably a throwback to my school

dorm days and the heady delights of cold baked beans eaten straight from the tin. I am also disgusted by the snobbery of certain grand restaurants who say it is non-U to give customers a side-plate. Where do you put those nasty little bits you don't want to eat? How do you butter your bread? Ignore this ruling totally.

Of course you'll expect to make money, but this is one thing I can't advise you on, as none of my own projects were exactly gold-mines. This was particularly true of La Roma, where the undergraduates saw no reason for paying, as all the wait-resses were in love with them. These dishy girls, whose six-layered starched petticoats could skim the froth from a cappuccino at five paces, were each and every one dedicated to seeing that Jasper or Jonathan got his free goulash.

Meanwhile, up in my crazy kitchen, I cooked with the help of not one, but two epileptics: Momma, a lovely old lady from the marmalade factory, who kept a mattress under the kitchen table in case she had a turn, and Keith, a six-foot student with a broken nose, who wore a crash helmet in case of further accidents. My cooking was basic. Apart from a goulash, there was spag bol at 2/6d – the students' favourite. Savoury pancakes were not so popular, as crafty customers knew too well the case history of these mini-dustbins. There was nearly always a skiffle group playing in the kitchen, while in the bar below the mighty Gaggia machine hissed and steamed, occasionally overflowing through the ceiling of Muriel's Modes below, ruining yet another consignment of hideous May Week hats.

One great advantage of running a restaurant is that you are never lonely. The students loved the warmth of my kitchen and roosted like chickens among the potato sacks, their noses stuck into Nietzsche, while young rakes from the science labs with Coke bottles of home-brewed mescalin sticking out of their duffel-coat pockets wandered in and out of the kitchen hallucinating on my bolognese sauce.

Happy days indeed. I can only hope that others drawn to this nutty profession will have as much fun as I did – and even, dare I say it, make a profit?

Out of SYNC

CLIVE DONNER's *first brush with the legendary film director* **DAVID LEAN** *could have been his last...*

After what seems an endless silence the handsome Augustan head is raised, and Britain's greatest film director explains what is on his mind. Anyone who ever worked with David Lean will tell you what it was like to be on the receiving end of those unreadable, unnerving silences. And yet he could be gentle, clear and supportive as well as utterly demolishing. The clarity of his explanations left no space for misunderstandings, especially with a script.

'Never, never,' Noël Coward told David, 'come out of the same hole twice', but after the success of *Great Expectations* Lean did just that. He decided his next film would be another Dickens novel, *Oliver Twist*. The four films before *Great Expectations* had all been Noël Coward subjects, and perhaps he needed to move on from Coward's influence and show he could be his own man. He had already become known as a perfectionist, at whatever cost.

In the early stages David worked on the script of *Oliver* with Stanley Haynes, a friend and colleague, and David's wife, Kay Walsh, an attractive and successful actress who had been closely involved with the writing of *Great Expectations*, and had been chosen to play Nancy in *Oliver*. David and Stanley went to a small pensione in Capri to sweat out the script. It was finished in four weeks, a record for David. Kay was working on the film *Vice Versa*, and among the boys on set was an urchin-faced kid from the Italia Conti Drama School called Anthony Newley. 'I've found your Artful Dodger,' Kay told David. The publicity department started a campaign to find a boy to play Oliver Twist. They produced 1,500 boys, but none of them satisfied David. Then they tested John Howard Davies, whose father was the film critic of the *Daily Express*. 'That,' David said, 'is my Oliver.'

Alec Guinness, a youthful, wide-eyed Herbert Pocket in *Great Expectations*, was convinced he should be cast as Fagin. David thought it impossible, finding him charming but lightweight. Alec worked with Stuart Freeborn, the make-up artist, and they showed the result to David. It might have taken him a long time to make a decision, but when Guinness presented himself in costume made up as the old skunk Fagin, even David's perfectionism was satisfied.

John Bryan's sets for *Oliver Twist* were inspired by Cruikshank, but also owed a nod to Gustave Doré, the French illustrator, as well as the Thameside warehouses with their sinister walkways high above the ground. The riverside warehouses were built on the back lot at Pinewood Studios and, with a bitter night wind blowing, a mass of extras assembled below, while the camera attached to the top of the rickety pile looked down on the Bill Sikes of Robert Newton – an actor much admired by David, with a well-known drink problem – and a cold and wide-eyed John Howard Davies.

When I first started work in the cutting rooms David was a remote figure. My first brush with him could have been my last. I was asked to get the day's rushes especially early from the laboratory, sync them up, and have them for him to see before he went on the set. He arrived in the viewing room bang on time and I gave the cue for the projectionist to start. Catastrophe! An assistant's worst nightmare! The reel was out of sync. I shot to the projection box, made the correction as fast as I could and ran it again properly. When I'd finished David got up to leave and I stood in front of him, my life in films in his hands. 'I'm very sorry, David. Dreadful mistake. I do apologise.' For the first time David looked at me as if I actually existed. His eyes locked on mine for a Lean Special. Then, after a pause, he said, 'Do it again and your balls will drop off.' I'd been given a second chance.

He had an instinct for knowing if a stranger came onto the studio stage without permission. He had huge ears and would pick up unwanted sounds in a flash.

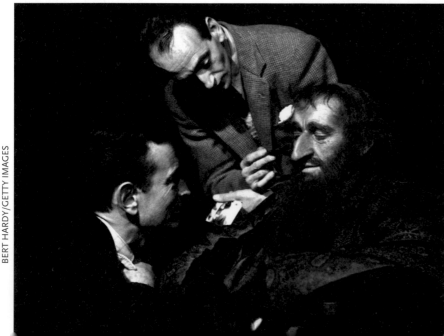

David Lean (left) directs a make-up session for Alec Guinness as Fagin in the 1948 film *Oliver Twist*

BERT HARDY/GETTY IMAGES

When work allowed, I would slip onto the stage to watch him, but he was aware of me at once. Sometimes he would beckon me over and explain in detail what lens he was using and why. Occasionally he would make me look through the camera and explain the difference between real life and what the camera saw. He was a generous and natural teacher. Later, I joined his cutting-room team and began what became a three-year apprenticeship. He was very patient, gentle and soft-spoken with his actors. He preferred to 'suggest' rather than to dictate what he wanted, though if an actor didn't deliver he could turn bitterly against him. When he found an actor he liked he hung on to him – witness Alec Guinness, who was also in *The Bridge on the River Kwai*, *Doctor Zhivago* and *A Passage to India*, and John Mills in *Hobson's Choice* and *Ryan's Daughter*.

David loathed Croydon, where he had grown up. He was backward at school, bad at sports, knock-kneed and pigeon-toed. He was in awe of his elder brother, who went to university and became a worldly success, while David developed a lifelong suspicion of intellectuals. But he loved cameras, and developing his own films. Eventually his father got him a job at Gaumont Studios. It was before sound, so rather than starting as a 'clapper boy', he simply held up a slate before each shot.

We went one evening to a private screening of *The Conquest of Everest*. When we came out into a dark and damp Wardour Street David headed straight for the nearest pub. After we'd been served and after the usual long silence, he turned to me and said, 'That's the kind of film I really want to make.' I was astonished, but he was a 'son of the Empire', born in 1908, nurtured by the *Boy's Own Paper* and the Great British Adventure.

> **David's eyes locked on mine for a Lean Special. 'Do it again,' he said, 'and your balls will drop off'**

Oliver Twist was the one film with which he had political problems. Alec Guinness's costume, make-up, voice and nose caused a great affront, and Jewish spokesmen in Europe and America argued that it aroused anti-Semitism. 'Being brought up a Quaker,' David said, 'I was blissfully ignorant of anti-Semitism.' Three years later it was released with twelve minutes missing, and only now can Americans see it as it was supposed to be.

Great Expectations won Oscars for Guy Green and John Bryan, directors of photography and art direction

respectively. David enjoyed seeing his crew being praised, but demanded great loyalty from them; they gave it him – or were dismissed. To George Pollock, his first assistant – responsible for smooth working on the set – he gave a gold cigarette case with the titles of the films they'd made together and the inscription, 'Please Sir, I want some more'. But David had to wait for his two Oscars – for *The Bridge on the River Kwai* and *Lawrence of Arabia*.

David asked Jocelyn Rickards if she would design the costumes for *Ryan's Daughter*. He wasn't comfortable with sketches but he refused to stop off in London on his way to Ireland to check on Sarah Miles's costumes. He didn't like them, but he couldn't explain why, or what he wanted instead. Every evening after shooting Sarah appeared in new clothes, and David would reject them. Nothing Jocelyn did pleased him, nor could he take criticism.

After three months struggling Jocelyn wrote a letter of resignation. She showed it to Steven Grimes, the production designer, and a friend and ally of them both. He read it, and turned white. 'He will never apologise to you.' 'I don't want an apology,' Jocelyn said, 'I want to go home.'

That evening, when everyone gathered for drinks, David made a startling speech to Jocelyn in front of the assembled crew. His behaviour had been appalling, his treatment of her had been rude and unjust, he realised she had only been trying to help him and his film. Jocelyn felt she had to accept such a fulsome and rare apology, and stayed to finish the film. Steven had hotfooted it to David and told him that if he didn't apologise Jocelyn would quit and the film would be in serious trouble. Years later, Jocelyn said, 'You know you behaved appallingly, don't you, David?' He looked perplexed and, after searching his memory, he said, 'I don't owe you money, do I, Jocelyn?' Everything else had gone from his mind.

I was fortunate to know David for much of his long life. In that time he became rich and famous, married six times, won two Oscars and was made a knight. But when I remember him I still think of those seemingly endless pauses in which – or so I like to think – the rich legacy of his films was conceived. In his head were his films. They were his life.

Yo *ho ho* and a lot of bottle

Pirate wench **ZENGA LONGMORE** *had a rum time in the pubs and clubs of Swansea*

Illustration by MARTIN HONEYSETT

Advertising executives have a stressful job. It must take days puzzling out how to squander their clients' money in the most innovative way. One of the ways in which they did so recently was to send a troupe of London-based actors into Swansea at vast expense to promote a spirit which shall be known as Pirate Evans Original Voyage Rum.

Never slow to get in on the action, I auditioned for the part of an Evansette. Evansettes were supposed to be the pirate wenches who would rush in a simpering horde on the heels of bearded Pirate Evans, the periwigged scourge of Swansea Bay. Charging madly into pubs, they were to hand out free rum, stick tattoos on all and sundry, shove free T-shirts around the place, then surge off to the next venue, leaving an unearthly quiet in their wake. Who would turn their noses up at such a job?

Swansea-ites, I was told, are very fond of chatting quietly about sport whilst drinking beer. The Evansette Experience would put an end to all this, and turn them one and all into a city of bucca-neering swiggers of Pirate Evans Rum.

Two things worried me at the audition. One was that the advertising company might cotton on to the fact that they could save on hotel bills and train fares by using local talent, instead of importing high-priced Equity actors to Swansea. The other, more pressing matter was that Evansettes were supposed to be blondes. Cunningly disguising the raven locks beneath a Marilyn Monroe wig, I was welcomed with a hearty cry from the auditioner:

'A Caribbean Evansette – brilliant! Pity you're blonde, but with a pirate headscarf, no one will notice. Welcome aboard, Evansette Zenga!'

The next thing I knew, I was being whisked off with a first-class ticket to Swansea, and sharing a double room in a motorway hotel with Tina, a fellow Evansette. Tina, a willowy Mancunian, had two topics of conversation which kept us amused far into the night. One was the amount of money she was able to earn in advertising (£200 for three hours' hard slog handing out cigars at celebrity awards), and the other was Manchester's culinary delicacies. Her choice favourites were Pasty Barns, a large bread roll with a meat pie filling, smothered in rich, nourishing gravy. Oven Bottoms were also able to render her misty-eyed. I never quite got to grips with what Oven Bottoms actually were, but I gleaned they had something to do with the jelly from pigs' trotters.

> **The mere pen cannot describe the uproarious bacchanal which is Swansea after dark**

Sadly for Tina, our company of thespians was taken out twice daily to restaurants where no self-respecting pig's trotter would dare display its jelly. Champagne, rare liqueurs and plates of unpronounceable food were edged towards us to an intolerable degree.

Much of the food remained untouched, the Evansettes all being on strange, faddy diets, but it didn't seem to matter. This was the world of advertising, where the hospitality budget ran into millions, so if you ordered a starter for £20, then decided you didn't care for the colour of the crockery, never mind, order another and leave that as well. A typical bill for a lunch for fifteen people ran up to £800.

Back at the hotel, the company picked up the tab for drinks, sandwiches and snacks, just in case any of us happened to get peckish between meals. The work came as something of a nasty jar, interfering as it did with the mire of gluttony into which we had all sunk.

The mere pen cannot describe the uproarious bacchanal which is Swansea after dark. Of quiet drinkers there were none. Hordes of women dressed in saucy bits of string, their exposed flesh blueing in the winter night, yelled with lascivious glee, followed by gangs of men, beer bottles waving aloft.

The pubs in which we worked fell neatly into two categories. Category A was the over-25s pub, noisy and frolicsome. Pirate Evans and his crew were welcomed with what amounted

to religious fervour. Well fortified with buckshee Cointreau, I whooped into my lines right on cue, just after Pirate Evans mumbled his 'Yo ho ho'.

'Ahoy, me hearties! We be the Evansettes, sailed into the fair town of Swansea to share with 'e our delicious Pirate Evans Rum, and give'e free T-shirts and tattoos!'

'What is this stuff?' I was frequently asked by a customer consuming his eighth shot. 'Whisky? Brandy? Tia Maria?' 'Something like that,' I'd reply. Not very professional, I do admit, but it must be remembered that I was invariably recovering from a champagne lunch.

'And where would you like your tattoo, sir?' I have previously lived a sheltered existence, and so will not divulge the most popular spot chosen to be decorated with the Pirate Evans motif. Most of the time, I was unable to decipher the South Welsh dialect, and ended up tattooing customers' ears with much difficulty.

I admired the Swansea-ites in the category A pubs. They had drive, and lacked the worldly cynicism of Londoners. I had hitherto only heard about Category B pubs from my younger nieces. Rake-thin, ashen-faced teenagers

swayed to bleeping, trance-inducing rhythms in the half-darkness. Their eyes bulged uncannily, drugs having removed every trace of natural emotion. Pirate Evans Rum and tattoos produced no flicker of concern. Occasionally a figure resembling a mummy recently emerged from a two-thousand-year fester in an out-of-the-way pyramid would stroke my arm, gazing with dilated pupils over my head: 'Gimme some of that stuff you gave me last night, like.'

I can imagine the mummy telling his dealer the next day, 'It were really good, man. I had this great trip! I saw a black woman dressed up as a pirate

'He's got your wrinkles!'

wench handing out free rum!'

Only the bouncers revealed a glimmer of human emotion. At one point, a black man was hurled into the street with Herculean force, landing head-first in the icy Swansea gutter. I swiftly concluded the poor man must have refused to buy drugs. None of the inmates so much as turned their heads to witness the blood-soaked youth pick himself up from the mud and slope off into the night.

There is a lot to be said for alcohol. It produces spicy conversation, rip-roaring spirit and smouldering glances between the sexes. Drugs, on the other hand, render the user a living corpse, incapable of speech and thought, every sense deadened. Perhaps drugs are a conspiracy by the Family Planning Association to curb the birth-rate among the young.

When you're next in Swansea, look into the pubs, both Category A and B, and tell me if everyone is now drinking Pirate Evans Original Voyage Rum. That way I'll know that the thousands of pounds thrown at the advertising campaign was money wisely spent, and not, as I sometimes suspect, merely an excuse to ship a handful of actors and advertising executives off for a riotous timber-shivering weekend.

Croc *shock*

*To lose one friend killed and eaten by a crocodile
may be regarded as a misfortune; to lose two...*

By **NICHOLAS WOLLASTON**

Illustrations by BYRON HUMPHRYS

Two of my friends, on opposite sides of the world, were killed and eaten by crocodiles.

One was Sam from Rochdale. He had been a tank-driver in the Irish Guards and couldn't settle back in civvy street as a garage mechanic. After brief stabs at various things, all too dull for such a man, he turned up in Uganda and got a job hunting crocodiles. He built a rough-and-ready camp beside the Semliki, one of Africa's great cocoa-brown rivers in the shadow of the Ruwenzori mountains – steamy, swampy, as far from Rochdale as possible – and soon he was an honorary game warden, famous and happy. When he wasn't hunting on the river he was up in the hills shooting buffalo meat for his men.

Once a month he drove up to Fort Portal to sell his crocodile skins. The day 'Semliki Sam' came to town the lights went up, the little place was painted red. He bought stores and ammunition and got monumentally drunk in the Mountains of the Moon hotel; and when the money was gone he loaded his truck with booze and sacks of salt for preserving more skins, before hitting the spectacularly tortuous road down to his riverside camp.

Far away on Lake Rukwa two English brothers with a team of Africans in canoes drove crocodiles into the shallows. Jumping overboard, some of the men grabbed a tail and lifted it out of the water while the others attacked the head with sledgehammers. On Lake Victoria crocodiles were caught in traps – a hook inside a decoy bird laid in an overhanging tree. The crocodile snapped at it and swallowed the hook, a heavy weight dropped and the croc was hoisted to its dangling death. But Sam used a rifle. It was cleaner, a soldier's killing.

I went to visit him, and got hopelessly bogged down in the swamp, thick black mud over the axles of my pick-up. The wheels spun, I sank deeper. But like a chief calling up his warriors – or an Irish Guardsman rallying his comrades – Sam had an instant gang of men with ropes to pull me out and tow me to his camp. The sun had dropped over the far bank of the Semliki into the Congo forest, the men skinned and salted the day's catch of crocodiles, Sam plucked a guinea fowl he had shot – and mosquitoes came out in clouds. The wattle-and-daub hut became a hive of hungering insects, and though we burnt smoke coils by the dozen the best defence was whisky. Outside, beyond the reeds, the river rolled past with a muffled gurgle on its way to join the Nile; and to songs from Rochdale's pubs and incoherent army limericks – and the whine of mosquitoes while the guinea fowl was stewing for supper – we drank ourselves into oblivion.

Six months later, out in his boat in the middle of the river, Sam was charged by a rogue hippo and overturned. The Semliki was deep and swift and Sam couldn't swim. Before his men could save him he was dragged down by a crocodile.

The other victim was Fitz, younger son of a duke, Old Etonian, bluest of the blue. We had sailed in the crew of a trading ketch from England round the world to the Solomon Islands: five months of tantalising lotus-island hopping between blank stretches of ocean. The lure of the South Seas wasn't a myth, and other wanderers we met had fallen for it: the Liverpool sailor in the Marquesas Islands who had jumped ship forty years before and subscribed to the *Evening Standard* to put him off going home; and the crazy New Zealander living alone off fish and coconuts on a tiny atoll in the Cooks

RANT

– he had seen nobody for six months since some pearl-fishers sailed away – and the Bristol engineer who had gone out to build a harbour in Samoa and stayed a lifetime: 'They say it's changed in England,' he said wistfully, but he didn't want to know.

In the Solomons I signed off from the crew and tried to confront the temptations. I could drift through the

> *He built a rough-and-ready camp beside the Semliki, one of Africa's great cocoa-brown rivers*

islands, pretending to be Gauguin or Robert Louis Stevenson or just a 'banana tourist', the scatterbrain who dreams of rattling palms and silver sands and big brown nipples, drunk with the simple life, escaping to emptiness. But it was the emptiness that frightened me and I got away in time, taking a cargo boat to Australia and a job as a jackeroo on a sheep station.

Fitz stayed on the ketch. He was twenty, he had nothing to go back to except London nightclubs and a smart marriage and now he saw a new horizon. Teaching himself navigation, he took over from me as bosun, and they spent a year trading among the islands: copra, mother-of-pearl, béche-de-mer, sometimes an impenetrable Chinese passenger or a Seventh Day Adventist missionary.

Then one day, fatally, they stopped to load copra at a big plantation, an outpost of the Unilever empire: miles of serried coconut palms, a wafting smell of future Lux and Sunlight soap, a magical anchorage. The manager, a one-eyed character from Sussex with a heroic war record and an entrancing wife, invited the crew ashore for a meal. They dined off fish from the lagoon, steak from Queensland, strawberries from Fiji, and over brandy and cigars the plantation workers treated them to a show of wild and whooping Polynesian dancing.

Afterwards, in the tropical night, with fireflies winking and cicadas ringing, with the Southern Cross lifting over the trees and young Fitz's blood rising to some romantic challenge and the desire to impress someone else's wife, he decided to swim out to the ketch while the rest of the crew rowed back in the dinghy.

He never got there. They waited and shouted and swept the river with torches, but Fitz was gone. Later his mangled bits, disgorged by one of the seagoing crocodiles of the Solomons, were washed ashore.

So there we are: two friends of mine, Semliki Sam and Bosun Fitz, unknown to each other, both caught and chewed up by hideous reptiles. And what's the message? Don't get too friendly with me, I suppose, if you're likely to go near a crocodile.

TAKE A LARGE pickled egg from a jar of brine (ignore sell-by date) and deposit inside a packet of salt and vinegar crisps. Shake bag, and eat contents immediately.

First introduced to me by my father at the bar of the Crown & Horns aged four years old, thus goes the recipe for the greatest pub snack of all time.

Of course, you won't find a jar of pickled eggs perched on top of the bar in most pubs these days. In fact, you'd be lucky to get a packet of crisps. Olives maybe. Or some fancy nuts dispensed at £5 a go. Pepper-stuffed olive inside a mound of Japanese rice crackers? Yuk.

I'm done with pubs. I've been going for as long as I can remember. But not any more. Like a number of people, I suspect, I just can't afford it. A pint is nearly four quid in my local now. Why bother when I can buy tins down at the newsagent for 75p?

Lager in pubs is disgusting. Why are the British incapable of getting fizzy beer cold? Go to a good hotel in Sydney and they keep bottles in buckets of iced water. Glasses, or 'schooners' – a more sensible sized 3/4 pint – are frozen in refrigerators.

Proper beer – or ale – is a joy when it's kept properly, but that's largely hit and miss. I used to enjoy draught Guinness, until I discovered several years ago it's inferior to the original stuff which you get in bottles.

Quiz night. DJ night. Cocktail night. Sky sodding Sports.

And the smell. The smoking ban means the stale aroma of nicotine has given way to the stench of industrial disinfectant. I haven't smoked for nine years now, but I'd take the fug of Embassy filters over that waft of NHS ward misery any day.

One for the road? Cheers. But I won't be stopping in.

HENRY DEEDES

ILLUSTRATION BY TOM PLANT

81

Indiscreetly *Frank*

The late Lord Longford had a holy thirst for publicity, says **JENNY MACKILLIGIN**

I knew Frank for twenty years and worked as his assistant for the last fifteen years of his life. I also visited prisoners with him and, on my own, went to court cases and helped to interview people for his books. I feel I know more about him than he knew about himself.

Our first office was in a damp cellar near Museum Street in Bloomsbury where he worked as a publisher until he was eighty. He had heard of these cheap premises in a local barber's shop, and having decided to turn himself into a charity in his retirement, installed his office there. The charity was called the Help Charitable Trust, which gave the impression that he would dispense money to the unfortunate when in fact he was looking for donations and only dispensed advice, lunch or tea. He used to pray in the lavatory, which was the dampest room in the very damp cellar – this is probably how he developed what he called 'bronchitis', which never really left him. One day, after we had been there about a year, three men descended the stairs and looked astonished to see Frank and his entourage at work in a well-furnished office complete with his family photographs. One of the men was the owner of the building and another a surveyor. The cellar was not supposed to be sublet, and we were squatting illegally. We left soon afterwards.

Frank wanted to stay near Soho and the Gay Hussar restaurant, and I suggested that a local Catholic church might give him a cheap room. I rang up a neighbouring church, which turned out to be French. Much to his astonishment, they had never heard of Frank. After lunch at the Gay Hussar, I pointed out that the church in Soho Square was a Catholic one, so we rang the bell. The priest who answered was called Father Pakenham – no relation – but he did not have a free room. We eventually

moved to a room in a boys' club in Shepherd's Bush, but this was not a success as the boys cut our telephone lines. Frank and I then worked from my flat until a month before he died.

He was fond of the sweet British sherry I provided, and of lunching at the Chelsea Arts Club, where he appreciated the gossip more than the gastronomic food. Once, while lunching there, I was annoyed with Frank for some reason and raised my voice. What I was saying was obviously overheard, as the next day the *Daily Star* reported that he had had an altercation with a woman in the Chelsea Arts Club. Of course he was pleased about this, but when I returned to the club there was a notice in the hall saying that it was a private club,

and that what happened there should not be reported in the newspapers.

One day, when the journalists were still in Fleet Street, Frank booked a table for lunch at El Vino. I always wore jeans to work and even went to the House of Lords in them. I did not know that El Vino had a rule against jeans, but Frank may have wanted to cause a stir. We asked for our table, only to be told my jeans were unacceptable. Frank called the manager and stood arguing with him for ten minutes in front of about fifty journalists. We then had our lunch elsewhere. Sure enough, what Frank had wanted happened. In the afternoon the *Evening Standard* rang up and there was a paragraph in the Londoner's Diary headed 'Earl Ousted in Fleet Street' because of his companion's blue jeans. That made Frank's day.

When journalists rang asking for an interview Frank would say, 'Whom do you work for?' If it was a tabloid unfavourable to Myra Hindley he would say 'No' – but half an hour later he was still talking, so they got their interview. Frank sought publicity because he thought it would further his good causes and campaigns. He did not believe in doing good by stealth.

Frank could be very indiscreet, but not out of malice. When he published a Prison Diary, he gave a launch party at the Irish Club. Soon afterwards he received a letter from some libel lawyers saying that most of the prisoners in the book had got together and were suing him for breach of confidentiality. They had not known that everything they told him would appear there. Frank was indignant and said that he had been writing books about prisoners for years with no problem: when the case came to court he was not going to hire a barrister but intended to defend himself. He was obviously looking forward to the occasion with all its publicity. But the case was settled out of court, on condition that the book was withdrawn. Frank once gave a launch party at the House of Lords for another of his books, this time on suffering. The first person he introduced me to was an ex-IRA bomber who had been in prison, now reformed. Frank had correctly given the Lords a guest list in advance, but the following morning he was jubilant to see on the front page of a tabloid: 'IRA BOMBER BOOZES IN THE HOUSE OF LORDS' and a description of the party.

Frank was xenophobic. He really did think that wogs began at Calais. There was a big country called Abroad which didn't concern him. He wouldn't go there. Twice he told me that he had to go to Paris for the weekend and that he was dreading it. The first time was because his son was number two in the embassy and he had been invited to attend some party. I thought it sounded romantic to be going to Paris for the weekend with his wife, but I think he was afraid he would not be recognised there. In London, if he was recognised but the person couldn't remember his name, he would say, 'I'm Lord Lucan.' The second trip to Paris was for the wedding of a granddaughter, who was marrying a man Frank called a 'Frenchie'.

I used to tease Frank by saying that he was a voyeur. He was not, of course, in the ordinary sense of the word, but his intense curiosity about every aspect of other people's lives could have made him seem like one. I once said that he should put 'Voyeur' under 'Occupation' in his passport. I suggested that if he were reincarnated he would come back either as a window cleaner, because he was a voyeur, or as a concierge,

'...the next morning the princess realised she was the victim of a horrible joke'

because he was a gossip. He sensibly chose the concierge.

Every year a friend of mine gave a birthday party for me in his flat, which Frank attended. Frank was told that one of my friend's lodgers came from Turkey.

'Oh,' said Frank. 'We have something in common. My father was killed by a Turk.' (His father had been killed at Gallipoli.)

Frank's *bête noire*, whom he referred to as the Prince of Darkness, was Michael Howard, then the Home Secretary. At a party in Downing Street a smiling, friendly man introduced himself as Michael Howard. Frank's immediate reaction was to cross himself.

Every year he took me to the opening of the Koestler exhibition of prisoners' art. He was not interested in art, but one year he took the trouble – with my help, as his eyes were already failing – to find a painting by one of his favourite prisoners, Eddie Richardson. It was of a fox peeping out from behind a dustbin. Frank said, 'The fox is Michael Howard and the dustbin is the prison system.'

M'LUD   **KATHRYN LAMB**

YOU ARE A WOMAN OF LOOSE MORALS, LURING LEADING PUBLIC FIGURES TO YOUR HOUSE OF ILL REPUTE, THEN EXPOSING THEM TO RIDICULE...

AND SELLING YOUR STORY FOR PROFIT. WHAT DO YOU HAVE TO SAY?

YOU LOOK DIFFERENT WITH YOUR WIG ON

Guess who's coming to
DINNER

Irresistible force **ELEANOR BERRY** *met immovable object* **BARBARA CARTLAND**
Illustrated by **ROBERT GEARY**

It was midsummer. I was about twenty years old. I had started to try my hand at writing but hadn't got very far. I was rather surprised to receive a formal invitation from Barbara Cartland, author of 325 books, with recorded overall sales of between 500 and 600 million copies.

She had invited me to her Hertfordshire house in time for dinner one Friday evening. When one is invited to a country house to dinner on a Friday, one automatically assumes that one is expected for the whole weekend, so I packed accordingly. I had never met Barbara Cartland and had no idea why she wanted me to go to her house. However, she knew members of my

mother's family, which may, for some reason, have prompted her to seek me out. There was also a possibility that she might have invited me by accident when intending to ask someone else.

I drove to her house from London. I extravagantly hired a black cab to drive in front of me while I followed – my map-reading skills are very poor. The taxi driver lost the way three times. The heat was overpowering. By the time we reached the house, both the taxi driver and I were in foul tempers.

I got out of the car and rang the bell. I was astounded by the fact that the door was opened by Barbara Cartland herself, who was dressed from head to toe in the brightly coloured fluff which

comprised her trademark. The expression on her face, framed by the shock of fairground-candy-floss-like hair, was unwelcoming. My initial reaction was of anger towards her for having dragged me all the way from London for no apparent reason.

'The name's Eleanor Berry,' I said abruptly. 'You asked me to come here. Here's the invitation card.' I sounded like an angry temp reporting to a personnel manager.

She continued to stare curiously at me. Eventually she spoke. 'Do you normally carry two suitcases when you are only invited to dinner?'

'Meaning no disrespect, any guest

assumes he/she is invited for the weekend if a card prints an invitation to a country dinner on a Friday night. Your house is a considerably long way from London and it's not really the done thing to expect a young woman to drive about in unfamiliar countryside at dangerously late hours of the night. I am quite sure that you wouldn't allow any of the heroines of your books to be turned out late, likely to lose their way trying to get back to London.'

She didn't say anything for a while and looked irritated. I had the impression that she was a silly, selfish clown who was messing me about. 'I repeat, you are only invited to dinner. I can't imagine what you intend to do with those suitcases,' she said.

'There's not much I can do, is there? I'll have to bring them into your house so that I can change for dinner.' She continued to stand in the doorway, while I waited outside. A funny thought suddenly came into my head. Robert Maxwell had once said that if someone treated me like that, I should hit them on the head with a shoe.

'What are you laughing at?' asked the Sugar Plum Fairy.

'Oh, nothing. I know that you are probably the most distinguished and prolific writer in the world, but (and I say this with the greatest respect) that doesn't give you licence to go out of your way to make someone feel as uncomfortable as this, when that person is only a girl!'

'Did you say your name was Eleanor Berry?' she asked.

'Yes.'

'And you're from London?'

'Yes. London's a *very* long way from here.' I uttered these words quite angrily. I was fed up with being made

> **Eventually she spoke. 'Do you normally carry two suitcases when you are only invited to dinner?'**

to stand outside like a bored soldier on parade. 'Miss Cartland!' I said. 'I've had enough of this. Do you want me to enter your house, or do you want me to return to London?'

She ushered me into the house and asked someone to direct me to a room where I could change. The room was almost as uninviting as the ill-mannered writer I had just met. The blinds were closed, and the double bed and chairs on either side of it were covered with dustsheets.

I stripped off and changed. The invitation card said that dinner was at 8.30. It was then only 7.45. I noticed a wall-to-wall bookshelf which contained only Barbara Cartland's books. I wasn't particularly familiar with them at the time. As I

had managed to get into the house and would be eating my (albeit thoughtless) hostess's dinner, I decided to be polite and on my best behaviour.

I looked briefly at the books, to get the general feel of them, so that I could express appreciation of them to their author, and finish her off with the opinion that I was well brought up. I took two out at random. Their titles were *The Wings of Ecstasy* and *The Proud Princess*. I opened them both at their front pages and put them back on the shelf, having memorised their titles. I took another one out, but can't remember its title. I found a passage which struck me as being almost as raving as its author: 'A woman wants to fantasise about the tall dark brooding man who crushes her like a flower to the medals on his chest.'

I sat next to Barbara Cartland at dinner. 'I'm an admirer of your books, Miss Cartland,' I said.

'Oh? Which ones?'

'*The Wings of Ecstasy* and *The Proud Princess*.'

'I'm pleased you liked them. What in particular did you like about them?'

'Well, from what I can remember – I haven't read them recently – I was struck by your vision of love in its purest form, rather than the tarnished and tacky infatuation which in this perilous modern world is mistaken for love.' I think she was put off by my academic language, which I used without thinking. She fixed me with a curious, vacant stare.

It has always been my theory that if you are a guest at someone's table, you have a duty to tell that person what he/she wants to hear, whether it is true or not. By the time I left, Barbara Cartland had become more pleasant and friendly towards me, possibly because I lied to her about my liking her books. I admired her because of the colossal number of books she had written, even if they didn't appeal to me. I learnt afterwards that she had done a lot of charity work, including campaigning for gypsies' rights. I also learnt about her background. She was the daughter of a Birmingham businessman who died penniless. She had nothing and was self-made. She started off by selling articles to gossip columns, before turning to romantic fiction.

The woman had guts all right. Of that there is no doubt. Where manners are concerned, that is another matter altogether.

'Sorry I'm late, I overslept'

THE BIG
FREEZE

'What a beautiful snowflake,' remarked **ELIZABETH BERRIDGE***'s husband. It was the first of many in the winter of 1947...*

Crawling precariously along the joists of our loft during the winter freeze-up in order to fill buckets with snow blown through the crevices of the roof tiles, I came upon a mound of cardboard boxes. These, together with rolls of carpets, old trunks and suitcases, made a lunar landscape rather beautiful in the gloom. Several packets had escaped a split folder and these I passed down to my husband, together with a bucket of snow.

Once the tank had been tucked up, with a small heater nearby, we investigated the packets. Letters, old manuscripts and several grimy notebooks: our mid-Wales journals for 1947.

We had moved on New Year's Day from a small cottage, without electric light or running water, to an old house with five attics and ten rooms. An icy day with a north wind, we had noted,

and a back door not properly fixed. We still had to rely on oil lamps for lighting, open fires or oil stoves for heating, but there was an open range in the kitchen, a resident ghost (which we heard but never saw and which frightened away several live-in home helps) and an erratic plumbing system. All for thirty shillings a week.

We had outgrown the cottage, which we loved, on the birth of our second child the previous year. And when, that winter, the pump had frozen and the nappies put to soak outside in a pail set like tripe in aspic, we jumped at the chance of renting the Squire's old Hall, empty for three years. At least we would have more room and hot water from taps and an indoor flushing lavatory. Luxury.

The first indication of the Big Freeze was on Llanymynech station in

mid-January as we waited for a train to Oswestry for our weekly shopping foray.

'What a beautiful snowflake,' said my husband. He was looking at my coat collar, where a crystalline flake of intricate pattern had gently landed out of a clear blue sky. It was the first of many, for the snow that had started so tentatively, as if testing the ground, went on and on, until the thaw in early May. From time to time during those months, six-foot-high drifts blocked the lanes, hedge to hedge.

Graham's entry for early March: 'Yesterday, armed with a spade, started out at 10 am with Tom Pugh to buy bread in the village. We dug our way across the field, then tunnelled along the lane through solid snow. Home again at 4 o'clock with half a sack of goodies.'

We struggled across fields so deep in snow that it came over the tops of our gum-boots, to fetch milk from the nearest farm, and loaded our two small children onto a home-made sledge to ferry back logs cut from fallen trees up the hill. A mixture of fun and necessity.

Mrs Richards, the farmer's wife, was concerned about the chilblains from which my daughter suffered and recommended dipping her fingers and toes in her chamber pot, then rubbing with lard. Had we enough paraffin for the oil lamps and stoves? Were we keeping the lamp chimneys clean and the wicks properly trimmed? Could people from London be trusted to do country things right? She'd send her husband across with a bag of coal and some more potatoes, and how about a few more eggs? This neighbourliness needed no urging from

government or radio. Because we were so isolated, people naturally helped us.

As the weeks went by, we adapted, as one does. The cruellest blow was a false thaw, followed by more blizzards, burying us deeper than ever. Snowdrops came out, then withered under the snow. Rabbits climbed five feet up the trees and began to eat the bark. Owls hunted by daylight. We tried to keep small birds alive by putting out food and water in a cleared patch of ground by the walnut tree outside the nursery window. Finches, tomtits, thrushes and blackbirds, all menaced by the strut of starlings and the bullying of rooks. And the silence was tangible.

At the village post office, where everyone met to exchange gossip and buy small groceries and rationed sweets, the news was bad. Dai from top farm had driven his animals into the stockyard and shot them, as he had

no feed left. Even worse, a farmer over Llangedwyn way had walked into a pond in despair and drowned under the ice. A tramp, our regular visitor between spikes (as workhouses used to be called), grilled his kipper over the fire in the pub snug and told how he had rescued the district nurse when she took a tumble off her bicycle on a treacherous hill path.

We had no car, no central heating, so life was simple with fewer things to go wrong. The attics were sound and smelt of apples, prowled over by our ghost. Was he cold up there, we wondered? Tom Pugh's wife taught me how to make leek and potato soup, bara brith and soda bread. We finished up the last of the sloe gin I had made in the summer.

We survived. We were lucky and we were young: this was the life we had chosen. We felt truly sorry for people in the towns, with burst pipes and no coal, stuck in trains and buses. Ironically, August 1947 was going to be a real sizzler: moorlands going up in flames after forty days of parching weather.

Over fifty years on we are a long way from that simple life, and the world's values have changed. Maybe it will take another Big Freeze to heed Thoreau's wise words: 'The cost of a thing is the amount of what I will call life which is required to be exchanged for it, immediately or in the long run.'

DEATH in the BALTIC

The Günter Grass novel 'Crabwalk' revived memories of a wartime massacre at sea, writes **RONALD PAYNE**

Half-forgotten nightmares of wartime death and destruction on the high seas stirred again in Germany with the publication of Günter Grass's documentary novel, *Crabwalk*. The plot centres on the sinking of the liner *Wilhelm Gustloff*, torpedoed in the Baltic by a Russian submarine in January 1945. The loss of the flagship of Hitler's 'Strength Through Joy' cruise fleet cost many more lives than the *Titanic* disaster. Less than a thousand of the nine thousand refugees who had struggled, fought or bribed their way aboard at Danzig were rescued from the ice-cold waters of the Baltic.

Many German refugees fleeing from the east as the vengeful Russian armies advanced into East Prussia saw the *Gustloff* as their final hope of escape. Most of them perished. So did the families of Nazi party grandees installed in their privileged cabins. Few of the four hundred women naval auxiliaries bedded down in what had been the liner's swimming pool got out alive. Places aboard had also been kept for a thousand freshly trained U-boat sailors, and with their destruction Admiral Doenitz's last hope of reviving his submarine offensive also perished.

All the luck seemed to be with the Russians. Captain Alexander Marinesko, the buccaneering commander of the S-13 that fired the three killer torpedoes, was an ace submarine warfare specialist. Yet he was already in trouble for disobeying orders from Red Banner Fleet command. Suspected by the commissars of lack of revolutionary enthusiasm, he lost his command. In mysterious circumstances, they stripped Marinesko of his rank and packed him off to a Soviet labour camp.

At any other time a *Gustloff*-size catastrophe would have provoked worldwide outrage and national sorrow, but in early 1945 this maritime massacre attracted small attention. It was under-reported, kept secret or ignored. Most Germans were overwhelmed by other momentous events as Hitler's Third Reich crumbled around them.

In *Crabwalk* Günter Grass focuses on the emotional dramas caused by the sinking: his fictional hero was born as his mother was being rescued from the liner. The fact that Grass concentrated on the suffering of Germans rather than on the sufferings that the Nazis inflicted upon others caused a stir in Germany. He broke a national literary taboo by reminding people of the horrors and misery created by the mass expulsion of Germans from the eastern territories.

This may well be a significant departure, but it is not the first book written about the fate of the *Wilhelm Gustloff*. Little was known in Germany about the sea disaster when, in the 1970s, I began seeking out survivors for a book on the subject. The extent of the disaster and the importance of the flight from the east became abundantly clear when, rather to my surprise, I found myself interviewing Admiral Doenitz, former commander of the U-boat fleets. In the final days he briefly became the successor to Hitler.

By this time a stiff and frail old man of 87, he lived in retirement in Aumühle, close to Hamburg. He proved to be a stickler for protocol and spent several minutes organising the seating arrangements for me and for his aide, Captain Reitsch. Only then did the old officer, straight-backed and formal in grey suit and white shirt, sit down himself. After offering us a sherry, he declared in a heavily accented voice, 'I vish to speak with Herr Payne in English – for twenty years I have not spoken English, but I vish to help him.'

And so he did, detailing how he had set in motion the great evacuation by sea westwards from Danzig and other Baltic ports. By January 1945 land routes westwards were closed by the all-conquering Russian Army. This was Hitler's Dunkirk. And Doenitz expressed pride at his success in rescuing almost two million Germans from falling into Russian hands. 'This made possible the postwar German miracle,' he claimed.

> **The *Wilhelm Gustloff*, once the pride and joy of Nazi tourists, began to plunge, boiling and gurgling, beneath the Baltic waters**

Doenitz's first objective in launching Operation Hannibal was to get back to west German ports the thousand U-boat sailors training at the naval base of Danzig. They were badly needed to crew the new Type 21 German submarines being readied for service. 'In December 1944 it was quite clear to me,' said the Admiral, 'that the main task for the German navy was no longer the U-boat war. All the naval force we had was to be assembled to save the people from the east and bring them back west. I asked Hitler to give me every merchant ship that floated.'

Among them was the *Wilhelm Gustloff*. This was a Nazi ship through and through, named in honour of a German Nazi living in Switzerland who was murdered by a Jewish student for distributing the *Protocols of the Elders of Zion*, the infamous anti-Semitic forgery. His widow launched the splendid new ship, built by Blohm & Voss in Hamburg.

The luxury Führer suite on B deck was set aside for the family of the *Kreisleiter* of Danzig. The final irony was that the Nazi ship lay in the port of the famous Danzig Corridor, one of the excuses for the 1939 German invasion of Poland. Now it was almost in range of Russian guns.

As the *Gustloff* was readied for sea on the evening of 22nd January 1945, its officers were unable to control the thousands of refugees who stormed the gangways. In the general confusion families were separated, mothers lost their children; babies were literally thrown to strangers on board by anxious parents. Just after midday on 30th January four tugs began pulling the *Gustloff* away from the berth and out towards the stormy open sea. As they cast off, the overcrowded liner heaved through the stiff chop of the freezing Baltic, bound for the western port of Stettin.

Shortly after 2300 hours Captain Alexander Marinesko locked his periscope onto the *Gustloff* and fired three torpedoes. The S-13's log recorded: '23.08: Three bow torpedoes fired at target's port side. All hit. 23.09: Target began to sink.' Aboard the stricken liner, panic erupted as refugees fought their way up from the lower decks. Anyone who fell was trampled to death. On the listing deck a surging mass of terrified passengers fought to get at the lifeboats. Others hurled themselves over the side and into the icy ocean below. As those fortunate enough to be in rafts and lifeboats looked on, the *Wilhelm Gustloff*, once the pride and joy of cruising Nazi tourists, began to plunge, boiling and gurgling, beneath the Baltic waters.

In the final moments the doom of the great liner seemed to anticipate, in a gaudy *Götterdämmerung* of the ocean, the end of the Hitlerian regime itself. As she went under, with boilers exploding, her emergency generators and lighting system were mysteriously and briefly reactivated. From her lifeboat, Ebbi von Maydell witnessed the extraordinary sight. 'Suddenly it seemed that every light in the ship had come on. People were still clinging to the rails. The whole vessel was blazing with light and her sirens sounded over the sea.'

'That doesn't look much like voluntary euthanasia to me, Mrs Forbes'

You can help change the future.

Here are the facts now...

- Epilepsy affects some 450,000 people in the UK.
- 30% of these people have epilepsy that cannot be controlled by drugs.
- Every year 1,000 people die as a result of epilepsy.

By leaving Epilepsy Research UK a gift in your will, or by making a donation, you will be funding ground-breaking research that will help change the future for people with epilepsy.

funding research changing lives

SCENIC *TOURS*
The Ultimate River Cruise Experience

SAVE
£1,000 PER COUPLE

Save £1,000 per couple on any 2014 *all-inclusive* luxury river cruise

When we say all-inclusive luxury, we mean it. Scenic Tours is the only river cruise operator to include everything in the price of your holiday; all meals in six onboard venues, all onboard drinks including your complimentary mini-bar, and every spectacular experience both on and off the ship.

Jewels of Europe
15-day luxury river cruise
Amsterdam to Budapest
WAS FROM ~~£3,245~~ PER PERSON
NOW FROM **£2,745** PER PERSON

Included: Award-winning cruises, with unrivalled local knowledge

We have one aim in mind; to bring you a river cruise you'll never forget. Our awards cabinet is crammed with accolades, including Telegraph Travel and British Travel Awards. It's why thousands of guests travel with us time and time again - listen to their stories at www.scenictours.co.uk

Included: Personal butler service on Europe's most luxurious ships

Relax in your spacious suite with a full-size balcony complete with sun lounge. All our guests now enjoy the service of their own personal butler*. No other river cruise offers this. Your butler will take care of your every wish, offering a full valet service and serving evening cocktails on your private balcony.

Gems of the Danube
8-day luxury river cruise
Nuremberg to Budapest
WAS FROM ~~£2,645~~ PER PERSON
NOW FROM **£2,145** PER PERSON

Included: All drinks and distinctive dining in our six onboard venues

We offer up to six onboard dining venues; Italian in Portobellos, a six-course tasting menu at Table La Rive**, or casual dining in the River Café. Better yet, all drinks are complimentary†, so a wide selection of wines with lunch and dinner or perhaps a nightcap from your mini-bar - enjoy, there's nothing more to pay.

Highlights of the Rhine
8-day luxury river cruise
Amsterdam to Basel
WAS FROM ~~£2,445~~ PER PERSON
NOW FROM **£1,945** PER PERSON

Included: Spectacular experiences in stunning locations

You're embarking on a true voyage of discovery; once-in-a-lifetime experiences that offer a unique and personal perspective you simply don't get on any other river cruise. And they're all included. Private concerts, performances and dinners set in breathtaking surroundings including gothic palaces and medieval castles.

LIMITED AVAILABILITY

Included: Everything... yes, everything

All flights from up to 16 UK airports, transfers in Europe, all tipping, WiFi and port taxes are included in the price you pay. With other companies, these 'little' extra costs can add up to several hundred pounds. At Scenic Tours, we offer luxurious ships, spectacular experiences, the most impeccable service, and it's all included in the price.

For your **FREE** brochure and DVD
0800 690 6379
www.scenictours.co.uk

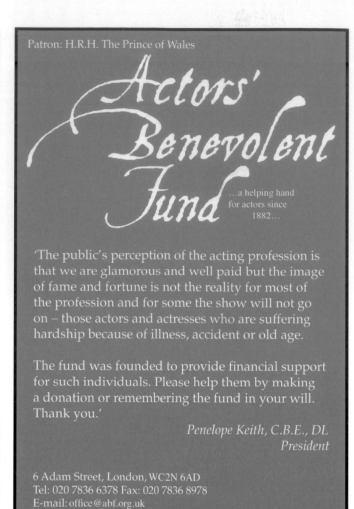

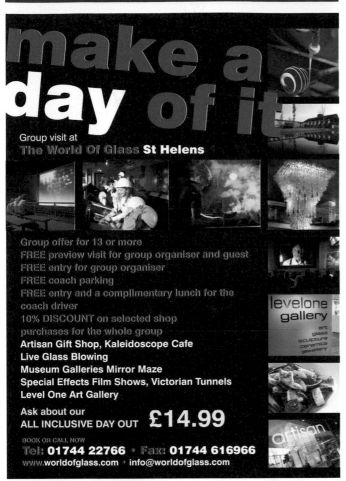

'He said "Bugger Bognor". Could someone fetch him?'